Twayne's New Critical Introductions
to Shakespeare

TROILUS AND
CRESSIDA

By the same author

'Othello' as Tragedy: Some Problems of Judgment and Feeling,
    1980

Twayne's New Critical Introductions
to Shakespeare

TROILUS AND CRESSIDA

Jane Adamson

TWAYNE PUBLISHERS · BOSTON

A Division of G. K. Hall & Co.

Published in the United States by Twayne Publishers,
division of G. K. Hall & Co.,
70 Lincoln Street, Boston, Massachusetts.

Published simultaneously in Great Britain by
The Harvester Press Limited,
16 Ship Street, Brighton, Sussex.

Library of Congress Cataloging-in-Publication Data

Adamson, Jane.
  Troilus and Cressida.

  Bibliography: p.
  Includes index.
  1. Shakespeare, William, 1564–1616. Troilus and
Cressida.   2. Troilus (Greek mythology) in literature.
I. Title.
PR2836.A85   1987   822.3'3   87–17713
ISBN 0–8057–8701–1
ISBN 0–8057–8704–6 (pbk)

To
Marjorie and Jonah Adamson,
my mother and father

Titles in the Series

GENERAL EDITOR: GRAHAM BRADSHAW

General Editor's Preface

The *New Critical Introductions to Shakespeare* series will include studies of all Shakespeare's plays, together with two volumes on the non-dramatic verse, and is designed to offer a challenge to all students of Shakespeare.

Each volume will be brief enough to read in an evening, but long enough to avoid those constraints which are inevitable in articles and short essays. Each contributor will develop a sustained critical reading of the play in question, which addresses those difficulties and critical disagreements which each play has generated.

Different plays present different problems, different challenges and excitements. In isolating these, each volume will present a preliminary survey of the play's stage history and critical reception. The volumes then provide a more extended discussion of these matters in the main text, and of matters relating to genre, textual problems and the use of source material, or to historical and theoretical issues. But here, rather than setting a row of dragons at the gate, we have assumed that 'background' should figure only as it emerges into a critical foreground; part of the critical endeavour is to establish, and sift, those issues which seem most pressing.

So, for example, when Shakespeare determined that *his* Othello and Desdemona should have no time to live together, or that Cordelia dies while Hermione survives, his

deliberate departures from his source material have a
critical significance which is often blurred, when discussed
in the context of lengthily detailed surveys of 'the sources'.
Alternatively, plays like *The Merchant of Venice* or *Measure
for Measure* show Shakespeare welding together different
'stories' from quite different sources, so that their relation
to each other becomes a matter for critical debate. And
Shakespeare's dramatic practice poses different critical
questions when we ask—or if we ask: few do—why
particular characters in a poetic drama speak only in verse
or only in prose; or when we try to engage with those recent,
dauntingly specialised and controversial textual studies
which set out to establish the evidence for authorial
revisions or joint authorship. We all read *King Lear* and
Macbeth, but we are not all textual critics; nor are textual
critics always able to show where their arguments have
critical consequences which concern us all.

Just as we are not all textual critics, we are not all linguists,
cultural anthropologists, psychoanalysts or New
Historicists. The diversity of contemporary approaches to
Shakespeare is unprecedented, enriching, bewildering. One
aim of this series is to represent what is illuminating in this
diversity. As the hastiest glance through the list of
contributors will confirm, the series does not attempt to 're-
read' Shakespeare by placing an ideological grid over the
text and reporting on whatever shows through. Nor would
the series' contributors always agree with each other's
arguments, or premisses; but each has been invited to
develop a sustained critical argument which will also
provide its own critical and historical context—by taking
account of those issues which have perplexed or divided
audiences, readers, and critics past and present.

Graham Bradshaw

Contents

Contents

Preface

Troilus and Cressida is far more absorbing and rewarding than any discursive account of it can be. Rather like Hector outfacing Achilles, the play outfaces the gazer:

> O, like a book of sport thou'lt read me o'er;
> But there's more in me than thou understand'st.
>
> (IV.v.239–40)

In trying to read and understand it I have found that it persistently resists one's attempts to sum up its potencies and define them lucidly, even as it continually fires one to try. This Introduction singles out certain aspects of the play as of special interest for anyone considering it as a dramatic whole: in particular, its extraordinary linguistic variety; its striking versatility in characterisation and scenic design; its wit; its changing moods and emphases as it unfolds; and its imaginative links and contrasts with many of Shakespeare's earlier and later plays. Because *Troilus* is so indefatigably self-reflexive, I have sought to weigh and use some of its own metadramatic terms, rather than importing similar but less satisfactory ones from recent critical theory.

My argument takes as its starting point the 'quarrels' and contentions expressed in and provoked by the play, as reflected in its bibliographical and textual history, its stage history and its critical reception—matters further discussed in the course of subsequent chapters, in which Shakespeare's use of various source-materials is also considered. Suggestions for further reading in these areas are set out below.

Various issues that have been extensively debated by modern scholars and remain the subject of much conjecture are not discussed here, or are touched on only in passing. Information on these issues is available in modern editions and commentaries: for example, the theory that *Troilus* was written for private performance at one of the Inns of Court; the play's putative association with the 'War of the Theatres', and its relationships with contemporary plays by Jonson, Marston and others; the complex issue of the many differences between the 1609 Quarto (the first published text of the play, a text now thought to derive directly from Shakespeare's 'foul papers') and the First Folio text of 1623 (now thought to have been based on a prompt-copy comprising a corrected and supplemented copy of the Quarto); and the related matter of Pandarus's final exit. In both Quarto and Folio the play ends with an exchange between Pandarus and Troilus, terminating in Pandarus's notoriously seedy 'epilogue', spoken directly to the audience. But the Folio also provides for an alternative last exit for Pandarus at the end of what later editors mark as Act 5 Scene 3. This seems to indicate an alternative version in which his appearance and epilogue at the end would be omitted, with the play closing on Troilus's 'hope of revenge' for Troy's 'inward woe'. Clearly, this alternative ending— quite often played on the modern stage—is less rancid than the 'epilogue' ending, shading the overall tone of the piece more towards 'tragedy', though not (in my view at least) making so vast a difference to the whole as is sometimes claimed.

Texts and Source Materials
Publication details of works cited are given in the bibliography on pp. 166–71.

Details of the play's unusual textual and bibliographical complications are given in all fully annotated modern editions, which also provide information and commentary on the play's sources, stage-history and critical interpretations. Recent editions include the new Arden, ed. Kenneth Palmer (1982), highly recommended, the Oxford edition by Kenneth Muir (1982), the edition by Stanley Wells and Gary Taylor in *William Shakespeare: The Complete Works*, Oxford (1986), and the New Penguin edition by R. A. Foakes (1987). The last two of these both appeared after this present Introduction was completed and in press. All these editions are eclectic. All except the one by Wells and Taylor take the Quarto as their control text. Wells and Taylor's edition is based on the Folio 'in the belief that this represents the play in its later ... form' as revised by Shakespeare himself (a process of revision which they believe involved his cancelling of Pandarus's appearance and epilogue at the end of the play, the inclusion of which in the Folio they regard as 'inadvertent', a printer's 'accident'). For those relatively unfamiliar with the play, the New Penguin's no-nonsense general introduction and lucid account of the text is a good starting-place; Anne Barton's short and pointed introduction to *Troilus* in the Riverside edition by G. Blakemore Evans is very helpful, as is Daniel Seltzer's in his *Signet Classic* edition. All these editions build on the earlier work of H. N. Hillebrand in the *New Variorum* edition and Alice Walker in the *New Cambridge*. The Quarto is well reproduced in the Oxford Shakespeare Quarto Facsimile series; and Charlton Hinman's is the best of various facsimiles of the First Folio. Two significant and relatively recent essays on textual and related matters are Gary Taylor's '*Troilus and Cressida*: Bibliography, Performance and Interpretation', which flutters the dovecotes in all three areas, and E.A.J. Honigmann's 'The Date and Revision of *Troilus and Cressida*'.

On Shakespeare's source materials Geoffrey Bullough and Kenneth Muir are valuable guides. Bullough prints excerpts from William Caxton's *Recuyell of the Historyes of Troye* (translated c. 1471 from the French prose-work by Raoul Lefevre) and from John Lydgate's *Troy Book* (first printed in 1512), as well as from others such as Chaucer's and Henryson's poems, Arthur Golding's translation (1567) of Ovid's *Metamorphoses* and Chapman's translation of Homer's *Iliad*. Standard editions of Chaucer's *Troilus and Criseyde* and Henryson's *The Testament of Cresseid* are *The Works of Geoffrey Chaucer*, ed. F.N. Robinson and *Robert Henryson—Poems*, ed. Charles Elliott. *Chapman's Homer*, ed. Allardyce Nicholl, gives the versions of the first two books as originally published in 1598 as *Seaven Books of the Iliades of Homere* (Books 1–2 and 7–11), as well as the heavily revised versions published in 1611. Richmond Lattimore, *The Iliad of Homer* is a fine modern translation. On the play's theatrical and literary background Robert Kimbrough's *Shakespeare's 'Troilus and Cressida' and its Setting* is most informative, and Ann Thompson's book, *Shakespeare's Chaucer: A Study in Literary Origins* gives the fullest commentary on that topic, which E. Talbot Donaldson has recently discussed in *The Swan at the Well: Shakespeare Reading Chaucer*.

Acknowledgements

I am indebted to the many editors and critics of *Troilus and Cressida*, especially to those critics whose views of the play differ most substantially from mine and who thus made it necessary to keep questioning the validity of contrary ideas. In trying to come at the play freshly I have kept the discussion unencumbered with notes while indicating where I concur with and diverge from others' views.

I am extremely grateful to the friends who read and commented helpfully on various chapters: Anne Cawsey, Ian Donaldson and Ann Loftus. My particular thanks are also due to the series' general editor, Graham Bradshaw, for his support and encouragement; and to Sue Roe and others at Harvester Press. To Sam Goldberg I am especially grateful for his constructive criticisms of an early draft.

In line with the other volumes in the series, all quotations from *Troilus and Cressida* and other Shakespearean plays are from *William Shakespeare, The Complete Works*, ed. Peter Alexander, London, 1951.

The Stage History
&
The Critical Reception

Publication details of works cited are given in the bibliography on pp. 166–71.

It is facile to regard the stage history of *Troilus and Cressida* as separate or separable from its critical reception: stage-productions and critical commentaries influence each other in many ways, direct and indirect. As discussed below in chapter one, there was little activity on either front until the twentieth century, when the experience and aftermath of savage wars, coinciding with the changes wrought in literary and theatrical tastes by modernist literature including Brechtian and absurdist drama, has engendered an unprecedented amount of interest in this abrasive, knotty, 'modern'-spirited play. Information about its stage history is provided in editions such as Kenneth Muir's *Oxford* (1982) and by Jeanne T. Newlin's stimulatingly tendentious essay discussing productions on the modern stage in England, Europe and the United States up until the late 1960s (1969). Since then, stage productions in many countries have continued to arouse great interest, the majority following the nowadays too infrequently questioned theatrical convention—overdue for reappraisal—of very strongly foregrounding all the scurrilous and degenerate elements in the play (as

epitomised in Thersites' diatribes) while down-playing
other elements that complicate and qualify its mordant anti-
idealist tone.

As in the theatre, so in its critical history, *Troilus* found
little favour until the twentieth century. Nowadays it is
widely admired and regarded as an important play in the
Shakespearean canon, yet its critical reception during the
past fifty years has remained full of controversy. Helpful
guides to the growing mass of critical opinion about it are
given by Kenneth Muir (1955); Ronald Berman (1965); John
Wilders (1973); and David Bevington (1978). *Troilus and
Cressida: A Casebook*, ed. Priscilla Martin, gives an excellent
selection of short extracts from early critics such as Dryden,
Johnson, Hazlitt, Coleridge, Swinburne and others (all of
whose views are discussed in this Introduction) as well as
from many twentieth-century critics. Two of the most
provocative and influential early modern studies that are
still well worth reading are G. Wilson Knight's in *The Wheel
of Fire* (1930), which exaggeratedly distinguishes the
'intuitive' Trojans from the 'intellectual' Greeks and
ignores the disturbing similarities between them; and Una
Ellis Fermor's powerfully argued study in *The Frontiers of
Drama* (1945), in which the play is seen as a profoundly
depressing version of a world in chaos, with the audience
being increasingly drawn to agree with Thersites. Another
essay that has similarly stood up well to the test of time is
I. A. Richards' '*Troilus and Cressida* and Plato' (1948).
Whereas Brian Morris (1959) stresses its 'tragic' aspects,
A. P. Rossiter in a packed, high-spirited essay (1961) sees it
as appealing throughout to a witty audience's cynical
delectation—a view taken further by Michael Long's finding
of breezy 'cheerful derision' in the play (1976).

Such diversity of interpretations has continued, with
opinion still dividing over the play's main focus and its
prevailing mood. For Arnold Stein in '*Troilus and Cressida*:
The Disjunctive Imagination' (1969), the thing is no joke but
like 'a nightmare we have somehow got used to'; by

deliberately keeping us at a distance the play's effect is one of 'uniformity of tone', with 'little variation in the range or depth of feelings'. Arguing against earlier studies of the play's language, T. McAlindon (1969) explores its stylistic clashes, its deliberate use of linguistic discord. John Bayley in *The Uses of Division* (1976), sees it as concentrating on the division of Cressida. Tinsley Helton writes well on 'Paradox and Hypothesis in *Troilus and Cressida*' (1977). Douglas Sprigge (1979) emphasises the brilliant staging of the betrayal scene. Douglas Cole in 'Myth and Anti-Myth: The Case of *Troilus and Cressida*' (1980), argues that its 'anti-mythic' method reveals 'a radical critique of human pretentiousness, a critique ultimately levelled at man's characteristic habit of myth-making', while Richard D. Fly in *Shakespeare's Mediated World* (1976), sees in it 'perhaps a critique of play-making in general'. Barbara Everett in 'The Inaction of *Troilus and Cressida*' (1982), draws attention to the strange 'storylessness', the 'analytical story-destroying wit' of 'this inactive play'.

During the 1980s others have added to this array of essays on particular aspects of the play, but to date there has been no extended critical study of the kind attempted here, which examines the play's unity in detail, and how it opens up, develops and drives to its violent close. Whether one knows *Troilus* well or is encountering it for the first time it continually baffles, surprises and disturbs. This Introduction concentrates on some of the ways it does so— for instance, the way it radically assails what Troilus fondly calls 'truth's simplicity', and the way its tough internal logic directs attention to the elements of illogic and anti-logic that prevail in its fictional world. While considering the design and spirit of individual scenes, my argument centres on questions of the play's dynamic structure and (related to that) its mixed, unstable moods. I have tried to keep questions of staging in mind throughout, in the belief that understanding how the drama works involves staying alert to its rich theatrical possibilities, even if only in the theatre

of one's mind. There is no universal foolproof method or
approach in understanding Shakespearean drama, and there
is no theory, however sophisticated, that can obviate the
need of keeping one's wits awake and thinking carefully and
feelingly about what Troilus calls 'th'attest of [one's] eyes
and ears'.

But of course different critics come at a play from
different angles, valuing and emphasising different aspects.
Many essays from the 1980s reflect the current proliferation
of diverse critical theories and approaches: Richard
Wheeler in *Shakespeare's Development and the Problem
Comedies* (1981) views *Troilus* in psychoanalytic terms;
Gayle Greene's 'Shakespeare's Cressida' (1980) is one of
many recent feminist readings; Jonathan Dollimore in
Radical Tragedy (1984) examines the play in its historical
context from a Marxist angle; and Elizabeth Freund
deconstructs it as 'Shakespeare's most daring experiment in
defensive self-presentation, and perhaps his noblest failure',
in 'Ariachne's Broken Woof': the Rhetoric of Citation in
Troilus and Cressida' (1985).

Other interesting essays in recent years include those by
Valerie Smith, Luke Spencer and others in a collection
entitled *Self and Society in Shakespeare: Essays on 'Troilus and
Cressida' and 'Measure for Measure'* (1982); by F. H.
Langman (1983); Juliet Dusinberre's '*Troilus and Cressida*
and the Definition of Beauty' (1983); Margaret J. Arnold's
'"Monsters in Love's Train": Euripides and Shakespeare's
Troilus and Cressida' (1984); Lawrence D. Green's '"We'll
dress him up in voices": The Rhetoric of Disjunction in
Troilus and Cressida' (1984); and 'Shakespeare and Chivalry'
by Ralph Berry, in his *Shakespeare and the Awareness of the
Audience* (1985).

The quarrel goes on.

· 1 ·

'And that's the quarrel'

The great legends of the war between the Greeks and the Trojans record unforgettably the propensity to fight. The gods at loggerheads amongst themselves supervise the two great armies pitched against each other, each side riven by internal disputes, individuals torn by conflicting emotions and desires. So it is appropriate that Shakespeare, inspired by all these quarrels, wrote a play that has kept people arguing with each other about it ever since. From one age to the next people have responded to *Troilus and Cressida* very differently, sometimes in quite contrary and irreconcilable ways. In our own century it has come to be prized and praised on terms unlike those in which previous generations have viewed it. It has also continued to provoke quite basic disagreements about its spirit, its genre, its effects and its worth.

What is the cause of all this discord? Why can't people settle their differences?

Shakespeare's play, like Homer's *Iliad*, which lies behind it, prompts the reflection that discord *is* a struggle to settle differences, each side bent on resolving the issue by opposing the other's will to resolve it on their terms. And there's the rub—or, rather, the crunch: the very terms in which the different parties conceive the issue are not merely incongruent, but actually conflict. Both see the situation and their own relation to it differently, each contradicting the other's basic grounds and premises. And the disputatious critical history of the play prompts similar reflections. It also suggests why any resolution to the debate in our time is bound to be highly provisional; and the likelihood is that the coming generations' views will be at odds with ours, just as ours are at odds with each other's and with our predecessors'.

Rather than fighting shy of such controversy, however, the best course is to include it in one's thinking from the start. By looking at some of the main bones of contention about the play, one can discover something about its own anatomy.

(i)

After a protracted debate, scholars now in the main agree that *Troilus* was written between 1598 and 1602, most probably nearer the later date, after the completion of *Hamlet*. An entry in the Stationers' Register in 1603 signals that 'Mr Robertes' intends to publish 'the booke of Troilus and Cresseda as yt is acted by my lo: Chamberlens Men'; but a familiar shadow fell between intention and achievement, and publication was delayed for years, as if to mimic the Trojan War. When the play at last appeared, in Quarto format, in 1609, the Quarto in its second state came equipped with a critical introduction—a breezy epistle headlined, 'A never writer, to an ever reader. News'. This declared in no uncertain terms that the 'new play' is a 'comedy' bound to please everyone who reads it, by virtue of its great 'dexterity and power of wit'. Exultantly, the 'never writer' tops these claims with the higher one that amongst all Shakespeare's comedies, 'there is none more witty than this'. Then he adds cunningly,

and had I time I would comment upon it, though I know it needs not (for so much as will make you think your testern well bestowed) but for so much worth, as even poor I know to be stuffed in it.

To an 'ever reader' coming upon it several centuries later this witty epistle, one and a half pages long, is still of lively interest. Of course there are questions that need to be asked about each of its many hints and claims. But even setting these aside, the epistle is intriguing in that it projects a conception both of the play and of its potential readership which, though doubtless skewed by the bias of the wish to sell, gives a clear indication—the only one we have—of how the play struck one or two contemporary admirers, or at least of how its publishers saw fit to advertise its merits and persuade buyers to spend their sixpences on the spot, at the Spread Eagle in St Paul's churchyard, over against the great north door.

The tone and tenor of the sales-pitch are in themselves revealing. In a hard-sell style it challenges a readership of witty sophisticates to prove themselves so by liking it, and climaxes in prayers for 'the states of their wits' healths, that will not praise it'. The epistle's exultant energy, its tough-nut stance, its aggressive confidence, all seem fired by its conviction that these are the play's own dominant qualities. An odd trick of its style, reminiscent of one of the play's, is to make its positive affirmations by thrusting through a thicket of negatives: 'Take this for a warning; and at the peril of your pleasure's loss and judgements, refuse not, nor like this the less for not being sullied with the smoky breath of the multitude'. In something of the play's own manner, it seems to get its gusto from pushing against whatever opposes, as if resistance is its enlivening force.

To the eye of hindsight, however, the most striking thing about the epistle is that its prediction that everyone who reads the play will enjoy and extol it proved, in the short run at least, so very wide of the mark. In the long run of the millennium it may yet prove more true than false: happily, the play is nowadays widely held in great esteem, and there is no sign of any wane in the high tide of interest in it. But this was far from always the case. Indeed, *Troilus* had to wait until the twentieth century to find many champions eager to embrace it as their own. During the first 300 years of its existence it was notably more of a miss than a hit, exciting little interest and less applause. Perhaps the diseases Pandarus bequeathes to the audience at the end of the play were more than their nervous constitutions could take, despite the 'never writer's' prayer for the safety of their wits' healths. For whatever reasons, his final phrase, 'will not praise it', ironically turned out to prophesy the critical reaction to the play more truly than his insistence that most certainly everyone *will*.

In Shakespeare's time, the public who flocked to see his other plays appear to have spurned *Troilus* and had little chance to see it on stage. It is thought that it was written for performance at one of the Inns of Court, but there is no record of any contemporary stage performance, although ambiguous textual evidence which indicates both public and private performances has attracted many scholarly quarrels, still continuing, about the circumstances of its staging, variations in the text played, and which came first (the latest theory being that private performance(s) preceded public one(s) at the Globe). It is not known what the young blades and others who bought copies in 1609 made of it. At all events, there appears to have been no general clamour or scramble for it. And this 'neglection' continued later in the century. One might have thought that a play much concerned with insubordination, armed combat, and the violent destruction of an older order, would have attracted fresh interest amongst those who lived through the Civil War and its aftermath; and that a play concerning a variety of illicit love-affairs might have been seized on gleefully by a generation especially fond of these. Yet when the theatres reopened after the Restoration, the demand for plays to stage evidently did not extend to this one, at least not in its original form, and an age which included such variously 'witty' writers as Marvell and Rochester (the latter of course particularly relishing the subject of sexual infidelities) either disregarded it or found it not to their liking.

The play's Prologue (whose lines had first been printed in the Folio version, which differed from the Quarto in various respects) had enjoined beholders to 'Like or find fault; do as your pleasures are'; and Dryden in 1676 liberally did as his pleasures were, by excising all the things he found fault with or did not like (including the Prologue), seeking to 'correct' the play and fit it to the best modern tastes. Dryden's version appeared under the title of *Troilus and Cressida, or Truth Found Too Late*. Advertised as a tragedy and quite unintentionally comical, this fascinating document is the most detailed evidence we have of a later seventeenth-century reader's reaction to the play. He found (as he explains in his preface) that Shakespeare's language in *Troilus* is rude and rusty, often 'ungrammatical', 'scarce intelligible', and 'his whole stile ... so pester'd with figurative expressions, that it is as affected as it is obscure'; so he 'undertook to remove that heap of Rubbish, under which many excellent thoughts lay wholly bury'd'. Not content with trash-removal, Dryden refurbishes with his own 'refined' diction. And these liberties with the language he extends to the whole design: he throws out such 'unnecessary persons' as Helen and Paris, reorders the scenes, adds many that are 'wholly altered' and many 'altogether new', amputates most of the war scenes and the 'philosophical' arguments, amplifies the love scenes, revamps the plot so that the play ends with all the right people properly dead (Cressida stabbed by her own hand, having only pretended to be unfaithful!), and concludes with some uplifting topical pieties from Ulysses, to the effect that 'since from homebred factions ruine springs,/Let subjects learn obedience to their Kings', plus a brief, obsequious epilogue from a would-be defiant Thersites. Despite some locally lively passages, it is hard to imagine a much more comprehensively uncomprehending redaction of the play. And therein lies its chief interest. By wreaking such havoc on Shakespeare's *Troilus* Dryden sends us back to it with a sharpened sense of why its poetry is indispensable, and of the imaginative force and logic of its peculiar design. His 'corrective' attitude to the play is remarkable partly because it so lacks any sceptical perspective on itself, any reflexive doubt about the absolute validity of its own valuations. But his unwavering conviction that he is right may jog us to scrutinise the grounds of our own critical preconceptions and assurances, and to recall that the play and the world can strike others very differently.

Throughout the eighteenth and nineteenth centuries, *Troilus* attracted little comment and no recorded stage performances (while *Truth Found Too Late* was staged several times in the century following its publication). Johnson, Coleridge, Hazlitt, Swinburne and others all had fine things to say in appreciation of what they nevertheless considered one of the most flawed, most difficult and 'least likeable' of all Shakespeare's plays. In general it was deemed an odd, unpleasant piece—and ignored.

But during the first half of the twentieth century, smiles of appreciation began to replace the frowns of dislike. At last, *Troilus* was put on stage in London in 1912, its first performance in England since the ones presumed to have been staged 300 years before. Other productions followed, and although then, as on later occasions, some were moved only to redeclare the play a failure, 'dull' and 'flawed', a growing interest in it was reflected by the more frequent stage performances during the next few decades, and by a marked escalation in the amount and heat of critical debate. In direct contrast to Dryden's view, it was now commonly regarded as a play about war with a skimpy love story attached (though, later on, the balance and relative importance of the two aspects again became a matter for dispute). This increased interest in the play, and particularly in its war scenes, obviously coincides with—is one expression of—the more general shift of outlook wrought by the experience of two world wars in which the sheer capacity for destruction, on a scale unprecedented in history, had brought into question the very bases and ideals of the social orders in the name of which this was used. It also coincides with a vogue for modern theatrical revampings of classical legends in a 'cynical' vein.

Yet far from now exciting more agreement about its nature, its significance and its merit, *Troilus* continued to provoke quarrels about its every aspect, and from the 1940s onwards the diversity of opinion about it grew greater than ever before. 'But how should this man, that makes me smile, make Hector angry?', asks Cressida, bemused (I.ii. 30); and the question applies, *mutatis mutandis*, to the play itself. In the last forty years, for example, many have seen it as a sardonic and highly entertaining exposé of bungling and ineptitude in love and war, whilst others have found it a much grimmer play, a deeply depressing vision of a world in which all values are shown to be discredited or destroyed. Some have stressed its cool 'intellectual' quality, while others have found its temper hotly scathing and rancorous, like Thersites'. Some have pointed to the immense creative energy of the writing, while others (or sometimes the same critics) have insisted that its spirit is 'destructive', 'negative', 'disillusioned', 'bitter', 'cynical'. In more and less sophisticated ways, many continue to link such claims (as they have been linked since the nineteenth century) to biographical speculations about the safety of Shakespeare's wits' health during an alleged black crisis of faith, while others continue to reject this diagnosis of the play's mood and to deny the legitimacy of such deductions about the life from the work.

Robust debate along these lines concerning the play's tone and spirit is only one aspect of the larger quarrel about the still more basic question, what manner of beast is this? After years of disputation the vexed question of its genre remains unresolved. The play is quite a nightmare for the tidy-minded. The Quarto's title page called it a 'History', the 'never writer' a 'comedy'; in the Folio edition, after a false start and a few more slips 'twixt cup and lip, it was put between the Histories and the Tragedies, the last of the plays to come off the press and only just in the nick of time, too late for its title to be included in the already printed Index. Twentieth-century critics have advanced countless arguments for and against all these classifications and other ones besides, such as 'tragi-comedy', 'satirical comedy', 'heroic farce', 'satirical tragedy' and 'problem play'—all of them terms that seem to beg more questions and raise more problems than they solve.

Naturally enough, these continuing quarrels about the play's nature—its form and its spirit—are bound up with the continuing debates about its value, about what the 'never writer' called such 'worth, as even poor I know to be stuffed in it'. In general the play is nowadays judged to have plenty of worth stuffed in it, and no other Shakespearian play has been so positively revalued in the last eighty-odd years, nor undergone a more striking reversal in its critical fortunes, from general rejection to widespread acclaim. Yet on the more specific questions as to what kind of 'worth' is in it, exactly, and quite how much 'worth' (in relation to others of Shakespeare's plays, for example), different people continue to make markedly different assessments, based on a wide diversity of grounds. Here again, however, in trying to judge such matters for oneself, it seems best to begin, not by attempting to weigh the merits of competing claims, but by considering what things in the drama itself can have prompted so many contrary and discrepant valuations. Why has it stirred such conflicting responses? Perhaps its worth partly consists in its power to do just that?

(ii)

To take the more basic question first: what is it that makes this play so quarrel-provoking, so hard to agree about—even with oneself?

One reason may well be that the sense of conflict in it is so radical and so all-pervading.

By 'sense of conflict' here I mean two interrelated things. One is that 'conflict' of various kinds—warfare, at-oddsness, hostilities, friction, division—is manifestly the play's main subject-matter, what it is *about*: the great 'quarrel' between Greeks and Trojans; the quarrels and factions within each separate community; fights and frictions between various individuals; conflicts *within* the individual person. As well as being 'about' this, however, *Troilus* is permeated with a 'sense of conflict' in even more fundamental ways, for conflict is as it were the informing principle of the play, evinced in its structure and its whole dramatic mode: in the kinds of dramatic language the characters are given to speak, for example, and the kinds of characters the play includes and the way it presents and contrasts them; the kinds of interactions they are shown to be involved in; the shaping of individual scenes; the arrangement of scenes and the incidents; the ways each speech, incident and scene is played off against others; and so on.

The sorts of conflicts the play concentrates on and which it manifests in its style and design are not, moreover, shown to be eventually reconciled, or even reconcilable. In its exploration of tensions and discordancies and at-oddsness the play is also exploring and expressing an urge towards their opposite—'harmony', 'unity', 'amity', at-oneness, 'married calm'. Yet throughout the play these possibilities are shown to be continually thwarted, achieved only momentarily, if at all, and 'no sooner got but lost'. However much (or little) they may be desired,the desire for them issues in further discord, which in the end is not and cannot be finally resolved. Pandarus in the opening scene asks, 'Will this gear ne'er be mended?'—will this business never be resolved?—and the ambiguity of his question neatly

combines the two great issues in which a long overdue
resolution is wished by all concerned: the 'cruel war'
between Trojans and Greeks over the fair queen Helen, and
the 'cruel battle' within Troilus' heart over the fair Cressida.
And from here the dramatic action moves, errantly yet
unerringly, via a baffling series of obstructions and setbacks,
to those two shattering scenes when these conflicts reach
their outcome in irreversible disaster. Neither is 'mended',
nor can it be resolved. Troilus, whose hopes all lay in
Cressida, now watching her betray him, cannot reconcile
the testimony of his 'eyes and ears' with the 'credence' in his
heart, and is heartbroken by the contradiction: 'this is, and
is not, Cressid'. The Trojans, whose hopes all lay in Hector,
now find he is hacked to death, his body dragged through
the 'shameful field', 'at the murderer's horse's tail'. And the
play ends with Troilus' unappeasable loathing of the
'coward' Achilles, and the cold comfort of 'hope of
revenge', not to heal but to 'hide our inward woe'. It is a
desolate ending for Troy, for Troilus and for the audience
who witness it. Yet even here any remedial catharsis of pity
and fear is checked and jarringly obtruded upon by the
incongruous wheezes of Pandarus, joking sickly about how
he'll 'sweat and seek about for eases', but ending his speech,
and the play, on the word 'diseases'.

To think of *Troilus* in these terms, as a play that expresses
a radical consciousness of radical conflict, is to think about
the discordancies within it, and the quarrels it provokes, in a
different light. This introduction tests the grounds for such a
view of the play and considers what these imply. Put thus
bluntly, they imply one thing in particular that needs to be
argued, though it cannot be proved: that this is the work of a
master-dramatist who knows very well what he is about. Far
from being the effects of ineptitude or mismanagement, the
play's notorious difficulties, on this account, are exactly
managed, wittily and wittingly designed. Quite what one
makes of a play so designed, and how one rates its
achievement and its limits, are further questions to think

about in due course. But one corollary of this view does need to be raised at the outset: if this play's very consciousness of the world is suffused with quarrel and tension, it will require of its audience a kind of imaginative patience as well as agility of mind—a readiness to keep the mind receptive to frictions and contradictions, rather than simply straining against them as things which ought not to be, or supposing that the play can be satisfactory only if it somehow resolves them.

(iii)

With *Troilus* as with any play, one's sense of the kind of drama it is and of some of its main concerns and interests begins to be shaped very early on, as we watch the opening scenes. The first person to appear is a figure clad in armour—'suited' (as he puts it) 'in like conditions as our argument', that is, garbed in a manner befitting the play's subject, the Trojan War. War being a matter of attack and defence, he presumably carries an offensive weapon as well as wearing gear to protect him, although his function here, as it happens, is not to fight but to inform. As he fills us in on some facts about 'the vaunt and firstlings of those broils', it is not just the facts but his manner of conveying them that arouses our interest and draws us in, for the grandiose fanfare style and urgent portentous rhythms of his speech catch something of the surging energy of the proud princes setting out from isles of Greece with their 'high blood chaf'd' and their ships 'Fraught with the ministers and instruments/Of cruel war'. His account speedily leaves behind even its own past tense ('have ... sent'), excitedly propelling itself into the immediacy of the now-unfolding present. As he tells how they leave the Athenian bay and 'Put forth toward Phrygia', and soon 'To Tenedos they come', the supercharged vitality of his language transmits the onward thrust of their journey, their gathering sense of heroic mission and of triumph within their powers, as they

'do ... disgorge/Their war-like fraughtage' and with spirits
high 'do pitch/ Their brave pavilions' on Dardan plains.

'Their vow is made/To ransack Troy', the Prologue
declares. His phrase registers the first shock of collision,
concussion, in the play: 'vow', a holy and safe-guarding
purpose or 'sanctimony' (to use Troilus' term), jars against
the desecrating violence of 'ransack'; and in that phrase,
'ransack Troy', the Greeks' reckless intention of wreckage
collides with Troy's redoubtable stone walls, the 'strong
immures' built to guard and defend her against ransackers.
Indeed, it is at those (so it seems) impenetrable defences that
the Prologue next directs our gaze, as soon as the Greeks
have pitched their tents, their temporary habitations: at the
ancient walls of the 'six-gated city' whose 'massy
staples/And corresponsive and fulfilling bolts,/Sperr up the
sons of Troy'.

The Prologue's function is to set 'the scene', before the
play 'leaps o'er' these 'firstlings' and plunges into 'the
middle' of the war. But in so doing, he evokes an image of
the 'chance of war' which casts its premonitory shadow over
everything that follows: an image or a possibility of
powerful energies surging forward to be met by something
that impedes or blocks them, or thrusts against them with
corresponsive force—an image of aims being checked or
obstructed by a barricade or an opposing will.

As the opening stretches of the play being to establish its
imaginative terms, to create its 'world' and stake out its
territory, this kind of situation—of aims being thwarted or
meeting resistence—recurs time and again. Discord and
frustration are everywhere in these first half-dozen scenes—
in the verse, in the characters, in the incidents presented,
and in the tensions between all these. On every side, in love
and in war, in personal and in public affairs, things seem
stagnant or at a point of *impasse*, stalemate. Many of the
Greeks' 'brave pavilions' now (according to Ulysses)
'stand/Hollow upon this plain, so many hollow factions',
the army no longer (in the Prologue's phrase) 'fresh and yet

unbruised' but stale and 'sick', unable to go forward except with Achilles' aid, just as Troilus, weary and bruised at heart, 'cannot come to Cressid but by Pandar', who isn't helping. Everyone wants to make something happen, to make a breakthrough, to achieve their desire; but everyone's will is blocked by someone else's. These opening scenes comprise a marvellous miscellany of minor quarrels and major altercations: battles of wits, tussles of will, squabbles and frays and formal challenges, orderly debates and pell-mell punch-ups, the outcome in most cases being either conditional or indeterminate, though everyone ends up more than ever determined to resolve the trouble as soon as possible on their own terms.

The run of these scenes is remarkable. They vary greatly in their pace and pitch, in their scope and their specific details, and this diversity is as striking as what they have in common. Something of this variableness is foreshadowed in the Prologue's rapid shifts of tone and diction—from 'the princes orgillous, their high blood chaf'd', to 'and that's the quarrel', 'Like or find fault'. Immediately following the Prologue, the play plunges from high heroics to down-in-the-dumps domesticity, crossness and complaint, with Troilus writhing in helpless self-pity and impatience at his lack of progress in wooing Cressida who, it seems, has a maddeningly maidenly will of her own, bent on being 'stubborn-chaste against all suit', while Pandarus cunningly fans the fire by appearing not to care. Having sent the young man into convulsive raptures of agony by referring to Cressida's fairness, and having perplexed him further by accusing him of being ungrateful ('What'? cries the amazed Troilus, 'art thou angry, Pandarus? What, with *me?*'), Pandarus then puts on a great display of tetchiness and non-cooperation, feigns complete indifference—'But what care I? ... tis all one to me'—and flounces off, apparently in high dudgeon, leaving Troilus prostrate and fretting with frustration—'O gods, how do you plague me!'—and aching with desire.

The following scene puts Pandarus into another cross-purpose duel of wills, this time with someone much less pliable than the inexpert Troilus, for Cressida is hardly 'skilless as unpractis'd infancy'. Her wily spirit of resilience comically marks her family resemblance to this uncle she can foil, and indeed she proves more than his match at sparring contests and ploys like these. She effortlessly wins the upper hand by wittily deflecting all his intrusions and resisting all his recommendations of Troilus' matchless merits, feigning indifference on that score and eager enthusiasm about everyone else, forcing Pandarus to push his case more and more directly in order to counter her sly evasions and parryings, which in the end she genially admits in an elaborate teasing jest about her need to 'defend ... defend ... defend'.

In its next four scenes (I.iii to II.iii, inclusive) the play switches from the love-affair on one and other side, Troilus' and Cressida's, to the war-affair 'on one and other side, Troyan and Greek'—to use the Prologue's phrase. But here too in each camp internal dissension not only impedes the war-effort but supersedes it, so that the great contest has been emasculated to a 'dull and long-continued truce' punctuated with minor 'sport' of skirmishes and reprisals, while the Greeks are engrossed in finding some way to make Achilles cooperate instead of sabotaging their campaign, and the Trojans argue over whether or not to cut their losses and end the war. The great combatants, like the lovers, are all oppressed by the burden of a situation whose outcome they must tarry for, and tarry, and tarry yet again: for it seems there's no end to what's 'yet in the word "hereafter"', if you would have your cake out of the wheat (cf. I.i. 15ff). They are all impatient as Troilus is, 'blench[ing] at suff'rance', all needing to believe like Thersites that 'I serve here voluntary', though indeed as Achilles bluntly remarks, 'Your last service was suff'rance; 'twas not voluntary. No man is beaten voluntary' (II.i. 92–4). But under these 'terms of base compulsion' they all exercise their freedom to dream, kick against whatever frustrates them, and endlessly entertain ideas about the 'hereafter'.

These Greek scenes early on, especially the council scene (I.iii) and its later sequel (II.iii), are immensely knotty, multifaceted, but the drama centres on the (for most of the time) conspicuously absent figure of Achilles, whose insubordination and intransigence have roused Ulysses' determination to bring this non-compliant giant back in line. The elaborate scheme Ulysses concocts to tame Achilles and make him conform involves harnessing his monstrous egoism by making him jealous of Ajax: instead of stymying the Greek generals by scorning them and refusing to collaborate, Achilles must be made to feel vexed by *their* disregard and scorn, and frustrated by not being coaxed or even invited to fight. Yet in the very scenes when this plan to subvert the subverter is being laid, other possibilities are also raised which cast doubt on whether Achilles will prove quite such putty in Ulysses' hands as Troilus is in Pandarus': Achilles is not just (like Cressida) alluringly 'stubborn ... against all suit', he is utterly recalcitrant, unbiddable, 'disobedient and refractory', 'an engine not portable'. Great stress is laid on his prodigious unruliness, his 'savage strangeness', and on the turbulent energies which Ulysses in his speech on 'degree' associates with the fearful image of universal 'chaos'. And this impression of Achilles as self-willed, perverse and unpredictable, chafes against Ulysses' complacent assurance that such 'raging appetites' can easily be curbed and 'physicked'. Indeed, this sanguine notion that Achilles and Ajax will 'med'cine' each other, or (as doddery Nestor puts it in his gleeful bit of doggerel about dogs) that 'Two curs shall tame each other: pride alone/Must tarre the mastiffs on, as 'twere their bone', also seems to grate against the contrary evidence which the next scene (II.i) underlines, when one of the said curs, Ajax, tries to bash the information he wants out of Thersites, who refuses to disgorge it. 'Pride alone' here only worsens the deadlock:

'Dog!', 'Thou bitch-wolf's son' ... 'You whoreson cur!' ...
'thou damned cur!'.

The sheer violence of this brawl—verbal violence and
physical violence—adds another dimension to the sense of
wrangling and animosity that the play is building up, for this
is the first time that, instead of arguing and trying to
negotiate, people have resorted to outright execrations and
thrashings, being at absolute loggerheads, neither side
yielding an inch, each goading the other to further extremes
of abuse. Beaten up by the brawny oaf he wilfully provoked,
Thersites retaliates with fantasies of watching Achilles
smashing Ajax to smithereens, pounding the daylights out
of him—'He would pun thee into shivers with his fist'. But
his only weapon is a punning 'wit' that is lost on his 'sodden-
witted' adversary, and the intervention of Achilles and
Pandarus can mollify neither party, for Ajax continues to
threaten Thersites, who continues to taunt, hiss and rage,
his only retort to appeals for 'peace' being to slam off, 'I will
see you hang'd like clotpoles ere I come any more to your
tents'. ('A good riddance', mutters Patroclus, but they are
not rid of him for long, despite this furious avowal.)

As the next scene opens, the stridencies of that fracas
seem even more extreme by contrast with the very different
tones and terms of this orderly argument, the Trojans'
debate about whether or not to proceed with the war. This
famous council scene (II.ii) is a crucial one for both the play
and the Trojans, and on both counts requires detailed
attention; but perhaps the most basic things that strike one
about it in this context are that, compared with the dogs
fighting over their bone, the Trojans here debate their issue
in a far more civilised 'rational' manner, though their bone
of contention is incomparably more significant. No less
than everything they value is at stake. And yet, by resolving
their argument as they do, and on quite irrational,
sentimental grounds, their decision here not only entails
further ferocious conflict but puts Troy at risk of being
totally obliterated.

(iv)

Even from so brief a glance at these opening stretches of the play it is clear that what it puts before us includes a diverse throng of conflicts, tensions and discordancies. But to notice this is also to notice that the powerful cumulative effect of these scenes depends on exactly how they are dramatised: the order in which they are presented, for example; the sequence in which the various incidents *within* each particular scene are presented; the specific language in which each detail of character or event is created and defined. And here too, a striking feature of these early scenes is that they seem designed to maximise the sense of tension and incongruity, to create a manifold impression of friction and dissonance. To what extent this carries over in the remainder of the play is a question which for the time being may be set aside; but since these first two Acts of the play establish the basis of one's sense of the whole, it is worth taking stock of a few details about how they are brought to life.

The order in which the scenes are presented is of great importance in all Shakespeare's plays, and especially so in this one, for it comprises the order of what may be called the 'dramatic action'. The audience or reader witnesses and experiences the scenes in *this* sequence; and in *Troilus* the 'action' incorporates and intertwines the two distinct 'plots' or story lines of the war and the love-affair, but is obviously not just identical with either or both of these. If the scenes were arranged in a different order (e.g. by grouping more Greek scenes together, followed by a group of love scenes, with less switching from plot to plot and camp to camp) this would not change the 'plots' but it *would* significantly change the dramatic action. Dryden prided himself on rearranging the play along these lines: 'I made with no small trouble, an Order and Connexion of all the Scenes ... [so that] there is a coherence of 'em with one another, and a dependence on the main design', he wrote; and it seems not

to have occurred to him that the original might be expressly
'designed' to *frustrate* the wish for such orderliness,
'coherence' and 'connexion'. Certainly, his reordering
smoothes out the very shifts and discontinuities which
Shakespeare's sequence seems bent on stressing, and those
disjunctions importantly influence the overall dramatic
effect.

Shakespeare's opening scene, for example, showing the
young Troilus stripping off his armour, sick of the war and
preoccupied with his love-throes, comes with an obviously
deliberate jolt straight after the Prologue, which promised a
grand military confrontation and made no mention of any
lovers, let alone ones like these. Troilus' somewhat Orsino-
like groaning and languishing over his unapproachable
beloved—Cressida, the pearl of India—are next sharply
played off against the second scene, showing the pearl of
India in person, chatting with her servant and jestfully
jousting with her uncle about the hairs in Troilus' youthful
chin: 'Alas, poor chin! Many a wart is richer'. Cressida's
soliloquy at the end of the scene, which reflects back
ironically on Troilus' and on her own firmness 'against all
suit', also provides the lead-in to the great Greek
conference, cast in a key and rhythm unlike any that have
come before. The Greeks' ponderous speeches would strike
one very differently if the play began with them (as in
Dryden's version), but as it is, their big talk comes over as
even more inflated by contrast with the small-talk in the
previous scene, just as in the first scene Troilus' exalted
ardours were contrasted with Pandarus' pragmatic
deflations about grinding, bolting, leavening, and so on.
And the scene showing the clash of wills between Ajax and
Thersites, which is pointedly placed between the Greeks'
war council and the Trojans' council, not only casts a
quizzical perspective back on Ulysses' remedial scheme and
forward to the Trojans' debate, but also continues to
reverberate discordantly when the high-minded, ardent
intellections of that debate are followed by another diatribe

from Thersites, wishing syphilis on the lot of them. This in turn is succeeded by further divisiveness and truculence, sneeringly summed up by that arch-quarreller: 'All the argument is a whore and a cuckold—a good quarrel to draw emulous factions and bleed to death upon. Now the dry serpigo on the subject, and war and lechery confound all!'— whereupon Achilles, who has previously upset the generals when he 'shent our messengers', again thoroughly 'confounds all' by refusing (in the flummoxed Agamemnon's hilarious phrase) to 'untent his person and share the air with us'.

The effects of these juxtapositions of one scene with another are in each case complex, not just a matter of simple ironical undercutting; and the same applies with the shaping of the individual scenes—the way each one is structured internally and as a whole. Here too, the relationships between one part of a scene and another often emphasise tensions and contradictions between them. The second scene, with Cressida, is a case in point. Her opening exchanges with her man-servant concerning the news from the battlefield establish the larger context of war and at-oddsness in which her own combative-defensive encounter with Pandarus then takes place: he bustles in on this conversation and muscles in on her private life, which she cannily keeps private by spry dissembling and bawdy patter, until the scene is interrupted again by Troilus' messenger-boy, asking Pandarus instantly to come. And his departure, leaving Cressida to herself (except for her servant who is standing off and not privy to her thinking-aloud) occasions an abrupt and signal change of tone, as, in a voice suddenly quiet and wistful, she admits her love for Troilus, and—in the next breath—her self-guarding plan to continue to 'hold off' and conceal her love, since although she reciprocates Troilus' love, she fears to lose it by disclosing her own.

The shaping of this second scene, clearly designed to accentuate the discrepancies between its component parts and to set up vibrations between them, is typical of these early scenes, each of which comprises a pointedly disparate series of exchanges. In many, as in this, a conversation or formal discussion is abruptly broken in upon by the sudden arrival of another person, or disrupted by a sudden departure, which alters the tenor and tone and rhythm of the scene. The Greeks' conference in I.iii, for instance, is rudely interrupted by a trumpet announcing the entrance of Aeneas and then by another louder blast to signal that Aeneas will proclaim Hector's challenge. The Trojans' orderly conference (II.ii) is even more rudely interrupted by the 'noise' and 'shriek' of Cassandra, who enters dishevelled 'with her haire about her eares' (as the Folio stage direction has it), an obtrusion whose jarring effect is increased, not lessened, by the fact that the Trojan princes themselves pay so little heed to it. And so on. The specific effects of each of these disruptions differ enormously, but the fact that the flow of the dialogue in these early scenes is so liable to be cut across or broken or deflected, sharpens the impression they create of things not chiming or running free—of a world full of cross-currents and incongruities.

This impression is further increased by the structuring of many scenes to include and stress some kind of contradiction, reversal or *volte-face*. Hector's startling turnaround in the Trojan council scene, when he suddenly agrees to go ahead with the war, having argued against this throughout the debate, is a famous example. His phrase, '*Yet ne'er the less,*/My spritely brethren, I propend to you/In resolution to keep Helen still', which turns back the tide of his previous inclinations, is reminiscent of Cressida's turning-back on herself (in the reverse direction, as it were), when the outflowing current of her love for Troilus is checked and sent the other way by '*Yet hold I off.*' But one of the most notable about-turns and one of the most arbitrary is Troilus' in the very first scene, when, having declared his intention to unarm and having just said 'I cannot fight upon this argument', he is met by Aeneas, who is on his way to the battlefield, and Troilus volunteers to join him: 'Come, go we then together'.

This rather glaring mismatch between the opening of the first scene and its close—between 'I'll unarm' and going off to fight—highlights Troilus' about-face, while leaving it unexplained; and many other such unexplained turnabouts occur during the following scenes. Just as, time and again, somebody's purposive will presses towards what it desires, only to be met by a stone wall of stubbornness or the countervailing push of another's will, so too that kind of to-and-fro, pro-and-con, yes-and-no, willy-nilly of contrary impulses is noticeable *within* individuals, one after another. In some, this contrariness takes the form of a simple (and highly effective) stratagem; for example, of blowing hot and cold simultaneously, as in Pandarus's well-calculated ruse of exacerbating Troilus' fervour by disclaiming further interest: meddling like mad, he insists that 'for my part, I'll not meddle nor make no farther'. (The great meddler in the opposite camp, Ulysses, displays the same *forte* later on.) The comical contradictions between what Pandarus says he 'will' and 'will not' do are brought out sharply: 'Faith, I'll not meddle in it. Let her be as she is ... She's a fool to stay behind her father. Let her to the Greeks; and so I'll tell her the next time I see her....' And of course the next time he sees her he neither lets her be as she is nor advises her to go to the Greeks; and his declared intent, 'I will leave all as I found it', proves both unfounded and *con*founded, as much by his own desires as by Cressida's. But in other cases the incongruence between what someone publicly avows and what they do is rather more strange and paradoxical, as when the inveterate stirrer, Thersites, raspingly declares 'I would have peace and quietness'. In his relations with everyone, Thersites' incessant itching and scratching and his obsessive talk about boils and plague-sores express his unappeasable desire for some appeasement, even as he aggravates his itches by rubbing them to get relief, jabbing at the scabs of old sores and breaking out continually in malign irritations. The dis-ease in him between 'will' and 'will not' or 'I would' and 'you cannot' is so acute that his self seems to *exist* only in chronic conflict, in being riled by everything, including himself.

Thersites is an extreme case. But in less acute forms most of the other characters in these scenes are also shown to be strangely at odds with themselves in one way or another. Agamemnon in the Greek council describes the drawn-out war as 'indeed, nought else/But the protractive trials of great Jove/To find persistive constancy in men'. But, pondering all these selves and the way they are presented, the impression one gets is rather that great Jove-Shakespeare is organising these protractive trials to test 'indeed, nought else' but the force of persistive *inconstancy* in men and women. Certainly, there is plenty of persistive constancy to be seen in the form of various sorts of cussedness; Achilles' pigheadedness, Agamemnon's doggedness, Thersites' obduracy, Ajax's inflexibility, Cressida's stubbornness, Ulysses' determination, Pandarus' pertinacity, and so forth. Yet the most persistively constant features of this world and the people in it seem to be conflict and changeableness. Even Troilus, whom one might suppose to be thoroughly 'persistive' and constant, proves irresolute and inconsistent on more than one occasion. Despite his intent to stay 'at home', some unaccountable impulse sends him off to engage in 'the sport abroad' which he had just been scorning; and this same young man who described himself as 'less valiant than the virgin in the night', and who claimed that 'I cannot fight upon this argument' over Helen, because 'it is too starv'd a subject for my sword', is later the one who most hotly urges the continuing of the war, on the grounds that Helen is 'a theme of honour and renown,/A spur to valiant and magnanimous deeds'. Conversely, Hector, having 'chid' his wife Andromache, challenges the Greeks to disprove that 'he hath a lady wiser, fairer, truer' than any of theirs; and then after this challenge is proclaimed expressly to rouse some action, he suddenly swings to arguing that the war should be abandoned, and then just as suddenly agrees to persist.

Faced with such contradictory behaviour it is obviously beside the point for the critic, audience, producer or actor to complain that the characters in this play are 'inconsistent', and equally inappropriate to try to gloss over the discrepancies, paper the cracks. The play makes very large demands on the audience's attention and on the actor's abilities (notoriously so, later on, in the case of Cressida), because it seems amongst other things to raise questions about the causes and implications of such volatilities and vacillations, and about how these are linked with the desire for satisfaction, stability, concord, unity; and also because it seems to raise even more basic questions, again in highly specific terms, about what constitutes the distinct individuality of a particular 'self', and about the amount and kinds of dividedness that a none the less integral self can contain. Which Troilus is the 'true' Troilus—the one who will fight or the one who will not? Which is, and is not, Hector? The one who says no, or the one who says yes? Similarly with Cressida. The second scene includes this ludicrous exchange:

> *Pandarus* Well, I say Troilus is Troilus.
> *Cressida* Then you say as I say, for I am sure he is not Hector.
> *Pandarus* No, nor Hector is not Troilus in some degrees.
> *Cressida* 'Tis just to each of them: he is himself.
> *Pandarus* Himself! Alas, poor Troilus! I would he were!
> *Cressida* So he is ... He is not Hector.
> *Pandarus* Himself! no, he's not himself. Would 'a were himself!
>
> (I.ii. 65ff)

And these questions of when a person is 'himself' (and if not, who is he?), and of what elements make him so, recur elsewhere. It is a source of amusement earlier in this same scene (I.ii. 12ff), for example, when Cressida's man replies to her curiousity about Ajax with his account of an amazing mongrel-man who hath 'robb'd many beasts of their particular additions', and who thus 'hath the joints of every thing; but everything ... out of joint'. As always, the details of this speech are significant, but not in this case as source of information about Ajax, for the cream of the jest is that this fantastic evocation of paradoxicalness and incongruence is quite incongruent with the Ajax who appears in later scenes. Not only are the characters in the play often 'out of joint' in themselves, but the descriptions they give of themselves and of one another—the very way they perceive and estimate their own or another's nature or worth—are often 'out of joint' with other evidence. And this cross-hatch of incongruity, which produces a great deal of mirth and laughter, also produces a great deal of bloodshed, tear-shed, pain.

(v)

The armed Prologue at the start, one recalls, had described the Greeks' aggressive propulsion towards Troy 'within whose strong immures/The ravish'd Helen, Menelaus' queen,/With wanton Paris sleeps—and that's the quarrel'. And in dramatising some of the subsidiary conflicts that ensue, the play itself in its opening scenes comes, as the Prologue does, 'suited/In like conditions as our argument'. Not only are its events and its characters conceived in terms of 'quarrel', but even the details of its language are 'suited/In like conditions' as its subject-matter, in that the play creates this world of conflict in language which (to use old Nestor's terms) 'doth sympathise,/And *with an accent tun'd in self-same key*/Retorts to chiding fortune' (I.iii. 52–4, my italics).

Nestor's word 'retorts' (or perhaps 'rechides') has itself been the subject of chiding and retort between textual scholars. But there is plenty of textually undisputed evidence of the play's accent being tuned in quarrelsome

key, if we keep on the look-out and (in Aeneas' phrase) 'set
[our] sense on the attentive bent'. Linguistically, the play is
highly adventurous, renowned for mounting fresh raids on
the inarticulate and for the booty it thereby wins in the form
of rich coinages and first-recorded usages, many of which
directly advance the 'argument': 'dividable', 'oppugnancy',
'abruption', 'rejoindure', 'deceptious', 'tortive', 'propend',
'assubjugate', 'multipotent', 'impair', 'violenteth',
'forthright' and others. The play also includes many words
that incorporate a strong negative affix or suffix, whose
negative/positive elements clash against each other and
strike a little spark of conflict within the word itself: words
such as 'disunite', 'disorb'd', 'dispraise', 'discredit',
'discomfort', 'disobedient', 'distaste', 'disjoin', 'disgrace'
and others. Similarly, many words take away with one hand
what they give with the other—'unclasp', 'unbodied',
'undo', 'unbruised', 'uncomprehensive', 'unfamed', 'ungain'd', 'untasted', 'unmingled', 'unsecret', 'untimber'd'
and the like—as do other self-negating forms such as
'formless', 'needless', 'bragless', 'languageless', 'importless', 'characterless', 'skilless', 'bloodless', 'brainless', and
(more dismayingly) 'handless', 'noseless'. Again, the
language is also 'fraught' with an awesome array of 'quarrel'
words—'broil', 'battle', 'annoyance', 'fraction', 'faction',
'swinge and rudeness' and so forth—and an even greater
array of terms of violence such as 'split', 'rive', 'rent',
'bruis'd', 'deracinate', 'enrage', 'strike', 'hacked', 'crush',
'frush', 'bloodied', 'batters', 'kill'.

But the sense of conflict pervades not only the vocabulary
but the play's very texture, the syntax of many speeches, the
juxtaposing of one kind of speech and another, one kind of
verse or prose and another. To be set 'on the attentive bent'
is to register the impact of all the contrasts between the petty
and the grand, the particular and the general, the abstract
and the physical, the knotty Latinate diction and phrasing
and the more blunt Anglo-Saxon terms, between the
sonorous and the gutteral, between great monolithic

speeches and quick-fire spats and brevities, between blank
verse of one kind and another and chiming couplets,
between verse and prose, between drolleries and heavy
solemnities, cries, sighs, outbursts of fury, chuckles, fear.
'What propugnation is in one man's valour/To stand the
push and enmity of those/This quarrel would excite? Yet, I
protest...', Paris says (II.ii. 136–8), in a speech and a scene
which marvellously display the energy of the play's poetry
and its 'flexure' and variableness.

In creating such a world of diverse and conflicting
energies—'propugnation', 'stand', 'push', 'enmity',
'quarrel', 'excite', 'protest'—the play's language is as
compressed and economical as it is varied. There is none
here of what Agamemnon calls 'matter needless, of
importless burden'. Every phrase and image, every speech
and exchange, works at once to create and define the
dramatic action: the play *itself* provides the audience with
the appropriate terms in which to apprehend it and think
about its significance. Agamemnon, for instance, in the
scene just referred to (I.iii) comes across as pompous and
prolix, but all of his apparently needless verbiage is matter
needful in the play. Like those of everyone else, his speeches
express and reveal his own particular nature: Agamemnon is
the person who sees the world and himself in these terms,
and who speaks of these matters in this and no other way.
Yet his words also have an 'import' and 'burden' that go
beyond the specific 'matter' of this specific moment,
because they take part of their significance from the larger
context not only of this council scene but of the previous
and subsequent scenes as well; and in so doing they also
impart significance *to* that larger context, by repercussing
with other suggestions likewise carried in the dramatic
language elsewhere.

An example of this is in his opening speech when he
declares that

checks and disasters
Grow in the veins of actions highest rear'd,
As knots, by the conflux of meeting sap,
Infects the sound pine, and diverts his grain
Tortive and errant from his course of growth.

(I.iii. 5–9)

With a command of logic all his own, Agamemnon
advances this ample proposition as part of his effort to cheer
up his jaundiced colleagues by explaining that there is no
cause for grief over the seven-year failure of their campaign.
But as well as revealing a great deal about Agamemnon
himself and his reading of the situation (matters to which we
must return), these words carry a charge of meaning that
reverberates through the drama as a whole. The full import
of these words is perhaps not wholly absorbed or realised
until the very end of the play; but even as Agamemnon
speaks them they begin to illumine and give sharper
definition to the previous and ensuing action. 'Conflux'—as
the editorial notes inform us—means 'confluence', the
flowing together of the 'meeting sap'; yet this whole image of
tides or streams of sap coming together and converging with
each other also powerfully suggests the opposite: the conflux, the flowing-against or counter-pressure of surging
energies that mutually check, resist and oppose each other,
colliding and forming 'knots' which 'infect' and 'divert' and
send the whole current 'tortive and errant'. And this idea of
'conflux'—a coming-together which involves conflict and
creates 'knots' 'in the veins'—is one whose ramifications,
tortive and errant, flow into and help determine the play's
own course of growth.

· 2 ·

'An edge of wit'

Troilus and Cressida is often called a 'philosophical' play—a
reputation that no doubt attracts as many people as it
daunts. Either way, though, it needs looking into carefully.
Hector in the Trojan council big-brotherishly censures Paris
and Troilus for commenting superficially 'on the cause and
question now in hand', and for being 'not much/Unlike
young men, whom Aristotle thought/Unfit to hear moral
philosophy'; and this prompts us to ask whether the play
itself (as distinct from the Princes) shows a more judicious
and profound grasp of the philosophical issues it raises. The
fact that it includes an unusual amount of abstract language
and rather abstruse analytical argumentation does not in
itself make it any more 'philosophical' than, say, the
Tragedies, nor any more profound than, say, the late
plays—even though it may sometimes seem so 'fathomless'
that one can scarcely (in Ulysses' phrase) 'find bottom in th'
uncomprehensive deeps'. Nor should the substance and
style of the play's own thinking be confused with its
characters' frequent philosophising, which is always biased
by their having a personal axe to grind and is often infested
with illogicalities. The distinction between the way the play
is 'thinking' and the way the characters think, feel, act and
express themselves is obviously a central one in all
Shakespeare's plays, though it works differently in each; and

28

it matters so much in *Troilus* that until one sees how it works here the play is bound to seem a bit perplexed—and even (as it has often been called) 'undramatic'.

(i)

It is not hard to understand why so many commentators have tended to regard some of the characters' pronouncements as the play's own. It is harder to be clear about what this misses and mistakes. Some well-known comments of Swinburne's shed some light on both matters (see A. G. Swinburne, *A Study of Shakespeare*, London [1880] 1929 p. 200). Greatly interested by the 'palpable perplexities' and 'patent splendours' of this 'political and philosophic and poetic problem, this hybrid and hundred-faced and hydra-headed prodigy', as he called it, Swinburne declared that *Troilus* 'at once defies and derides all definitive comment'; yet in his next breath, daring to be defied and derided, he comments, 'This however we may surely and confidently say of it, that of all Shakespeare's offspring it is the one whose best things lose least by extraction and separation from their context'.

By 'best things' Swinburne evidently means maxims, *bon mots*, dicta, what Pandarus calls 'goodly sayings' (IV.iv. 14). Yet even on this diminished definition some of the 'best things' in the play suggest, on the contrary, that it is foolhardy to be off one's guard in this fashion, to lapse into confident 'surety secure'. As Hector says, 'modest doubt is call'd/The beacon of the wise'—a point that neatly illustrates both the truth and the falsity of Swinburne's claim. On the one side, yes, even if lifted from its context, Hector's dictum remains a fine discrete sentiment—as is the case (to take an example on a much larger scale) with Ulysses' long admonitory speech about Time having 'a wallet at his back,/Wherein he puts alms for oblivion' (III.iii. 145ff). On the other side, no, these things lose so much if they are extracted from their context that they effectively cease to be 'best things', however memorably expressed, and are reduced to inert *sententiae*, disembodied truths or truisms. In its context in the Trojan council, for instance, Hector's remark not only expresses a general truth, but more particularly expresses his own wise caution in opposing the recklessness of his 'madly hot' brothers; and in doing that it also underlines—in a way he himself is unconscious of—the mad illogic of his subsequent change of tune. 'Modest doubt' is precisely what Hector throws overboard at the end of this scene, and it is what he again disastrously forgets later on, when he trusts that his enemies won't attack an unarmed man.

Troilus is full of quotable quotes, brief and long: 'Things won are done; joy's soul lies in the doing'; 'In the reproof of chance/Lies the true proof of men'; 'The elephant hath joints, but none for courtesy; his legs are for necessity, not for flexure'; 'To fear the worst oft cures the worse'; 'things in motion sooner catch the eye/Than what stirs not'—and so on. But enjoying these eloquent gems as gems, detached fragments, pearls of wisdom, is not the same as grasping their significance in the play. Extractive criticism loses touch with Shakespeare's dramatic procedure and distorts the play by de-dramatising it, because it disregards the key fact: that the drama presents a specific range of individual characters in specific situations and relationships—not a collection of free-floating 'ideas', 'themes', theses, commonplaces or what-not. Most of the characters in *Troilus* occasionally or frequently speak in terms that are very general, often universal, and often abstract; but their speeches none the less vividly reveal their individual natures, and in every scene the questions of who says what, and to whom, and when, and who else says what, make all the difference. No matter how general or abstract the language, the drama in *Troilus* is extremely particular.

The classic examples here of course are the two great

council scenes—the Greeks' in I.iii and the Trojans' in II.ii—which critics used to be very fond of extracting from context and then further extracting bits from them, often citing these as the play's key ideas. Ulysses' great speech on 'degree', for instance (I.iii. 75ff) and Troilus' question, 'What's aught but as 'tis valued?' were commonly discussed as if they came, not from Ulysses and Troilus, but straight from the horse's mouth—as if they were Shakespeare's or the play's own views, expressed through the character-as-mouthpiece. No one seeing the play on stage could hold to this notion for long, however, or suppose that these speeches are presented 'straight', without any complicating ironical perspective on them. Nowadays this is generally recognised, and critics are happily more apt to think of plays as works designed to be seen and heard on the stage, which therefore require to be so seen and heard in the 'theatre' of the reader's imagination as well. Doing this certainly prevents one from thinking of the words as if they occurred in a vacuum, spoken by no one in particular, or as if they issued from a mouthpiece: what we witness and hear is this and that *person*, saying this and that.

For example—to leap over the play's vaunt and firstlings to the middle for a minute—consider the speech that Troilus makes at that long-awaited moment when to all three's fluttering excitement Pandarus is about to bring the lovers together. Troilus is nearly delirious with anticipation, and left alone for a few minutes he breaks into an extraordinary speech of rapt expectancy. This is one of the high-points of the play, and as funny as it is touching. Even if 'separated and extracted from its context' this could never be mistaken for a speech by Diomedes, say, or Pandarus or Hector—nor, for that matter by Romeo, or Antony, or Florizel in *The Winter's Tale*. It is quintessentially Troilus' speech—distinctive of him and no other person, and in being so, distinctive of this and no other play:

Pandarus   Walk here i'th' orchard, I'll bring her
             straight.
[Exit]

Troilus   I am giddy; expectation whirls me round.
             Th'imaginary relish is so sweet
             That it enchants my sense; what will it be
             When that the wat'ry palate tastes indeed
             Love's thrice-repured nectar? Death, I fear
                  me,
             Swooning destruction, or some joy too fine,
             Too subtle-potent, tun'd too sharp in
                  sweetness,
             For the capacity of my ruder powers.
             I fear it much; and I do fear besides
             That I shall lose distinction in my joys,
             As doth a battle, when they charge on heaps
             The enemy flying.
                  [Re-enter Pandarus]
                                          (III.ii. 16–28)

On the brink of the great unknown, Troilus giddily whirls
in wonder at what it will be: he is stalking about the door of
the experience, 'staying for waftage', as he breathlessly puts
it, for 'swift transportance' and wings to fly over the Stygian
river of oblivion to where he will know and 'taste indeed'
what he has dreamed of all these weary months. He cannot
yet know this ecstasy, but he can imagine it with an
imagination excitable enough to make his palate water, and
his expectations are wholly shaped by the pressure of his
longings and fears. With not much in his experience to go
on, he goes on the most exotic things he can think of—
'wallowing' in 'lily beds', tasting 'nectar' from fruits of the
orchard where he waits, but nectar 'thrice-repured', beyond
a man's saying sweet. Charged with all the intensity of his
desire for immediate sensual gratification, the 'imaginary

relish' of it makes it seem in prospect perhaps too exquisite to be savoured to the full; and the mingled thrill and fear of this make his heart beat 'thicker than a feverous pulse'— fearing that his palate won't be fine enough to tell one degree of sweetness from another, and that his 'ruder powers' may lack 'capacity' to meet the swooning blackout of 'death'. Thus, in his fear that his joy may be too fine and that he may 'lose distinction'—startlingly expressed in his image of violent obliteration in a battle charge—Troilus' speech implies his consciousness of a possible discrepancy between 'the imaginary relish' and the 'taste indeed'. But his sharp desire shapes even his sense of this, for he imagines only that the nectar may far exceed his great expectations; he has no glimmering that it might fall short or perhaps quite fail in the promised sweetness. The idea doesn't cross his mind, which Cressida in the first scene takes for granted, that 'love got' may turn out to be less 'sweet' than 'when desire did sue'.

And it is characteristic of this restless Troilus, whose present moments seem always to be filled with anxiety about future ones, that when Cressida at last comes and he tastes her lips indeed, his mind instantly flies off to an ideal dream-world where this would last forever in an eternally persistive constancy:

Troilus   O that I thought it could be in a woman—
As, if it can, I will presume in you—
To feed for aye her lamp and flames of love;
To keep her constancy in plight and youth,
Outliving beauty's outward, with a mind
That doth renew swifter than blood decays!
Or that persuasion could but thus convince
   me
That my integrity and truth to you
Might be affronted with the match and
   weight
Of such a winnowed purity in love.
How were I then uplifted! but, alas,

> I am as true as truth's simplicity,
> And simpler than the infancy of truth!
>
> (III.ii. 154–66)

As it happens—or, more accurately, as Shakespeare dramatically presents it—Troilus' speeches in this scene tellingly echo some of the same terms used by others in earlier scenes. When he speaks of his fear that he may 'lose distinction', for example, or wishes for 'winnowed purity', his words re-echo those of Agamemnon and Ulysses in the Greek council scene. Such reverberations are another persistive feature of the drama. The characters' necessary unawareness of them does not curtail their significance, but is part of it. Much of the play's piquancy comes from the ways it capitalises on the gaps between its own apprehensions and theirs: by revealing discrepancies between one person's sense of himself and others' sense of him, for instance, or between different people's conceptions of their current situation, or between a person's words and his or her deeds, or between his particular (private or public) concerns in a given speech and the larger impersonal bearings and significance of the language in which he utters them.

(ii)

The Greek council scene, for instance, is arranged so as to highlight the links and the differences between the various participants' ideas and opinions about the war's stalemate. Many of the speeches are cast in very general terms, but here as always what Dr Johnson in his Notes on the play called the 'great variety' and 'great exactness' of the characterisation is very important. Each of the Greeks has his own concerns, his own way of talking, his own kind of public rhetoric; and his every speech expresses his disposition and cast of mind as distinctly as, say, Cressida's

speeches manifest hers in the scene just before. Her
soliloquy at the end of that scene in fact reveals something of
her particular nature in terms which now carry over into the
council scene, when on the basis of some general
propositions (which strike us as questionable) she
concludes roundly, 'Therefore this maxim out of love I
teach:/Achievement is command; ungain'd, beseech'.

Straight after this the play presents the Greek com-
manders discussing their dismal non-'achievement' in the
war. Agamemnon opens the proceedings by dealing with
things 'ungain'd' in a highly idiosyncratic way, maintaining
that there's nothing to feel glum about in the least. Not for
him the depressions of the lugubrious King in *Henry IV*, for
instance ('So shaken as we are, so wan with care ...'). Quite
unshaken, Agamemnon can't see what the Princes are
grieved about, and he intends at once to dispel their gloom
and boost their morale. The 'high and mighty' 'great
commander' seems a touch like young Lysander in the
opening scene of *A Midsummer Night's Dream*, who turns to
Hermia, suddenly under penalty of death or the convent,
with 'How now, my love! Why is your cheek so pale?'. Thus
Agamemnon:

> Princes,
> What grief hath set these jaundies o'er your cheeks?
> The ample proposition that hope makes
> In all designs begun on earth below
> Fails in the promis'd largeness.
>
> (I.iii. 1–5)

The great general is a great generaliser, it seems—the
particular type who has very little interest in particulars.
Phrase after phrase holds out vast, vague, encouraging
prospects: 'ample proposition', 'hope', 'makes', 'all
designs', 'begun', 'promis'd largeness'; and it seems that
Agamemnon is not the man to let a mere detail like 'fail' bar
his way or check his sanguinity. To be sure, his negative

verb, 'fails', is stressed by the syntax and rhythms of his speech, but his soothing tones and coaxing emphasis on '*all* designs' effectively render it calmly *un*stressful: 'fails' is smoothly neutralised and tamed into a benign, mundane, unlamentable part of life. And indeed, all through his long speech, rather than letting failure, 'checks', 'disasters' and suchlike demolish or even slightly damage the comfortably furnished tent of his optimism, Agamemnon makes them serve as its trusty framework, the very things which secure it against any future ill-winds that might blow. Fiascos of one sort or another, he contends, inhere in the very nature of things, inevitably and unavoidably, as past history also goes to show; and to suppose that we Princes need feel abashed or in any way responsible for the miscarriage of 'our works' is to misconstrue the situation altogether.

In view of what the situation *is*—'after seven years' siege yet Troy walls stand'—there's a certain genius in the way Agamemnon construes all the facts to fit his will, renaming shame as a cause for self-congratulation and treating total failure as the warrant of success. All negatives are revalued as positives; nothing impedes the flow of his assurance that they'll soon be tasting indeed the sweets of success; and in the meantime, he suggests, the generals' only sensible course of action is to sit about and wait. But the real genius behind all this, of course, is the dramatist's. With marvellous deftness Shakespeare reveals Agamemnon's attempt at tactical rhetoric as a species of self-gulling woolly-mindedness. Every phrase lays bare the general's muddle-headed wishful thinking, and thus exposed, his 'evasion'—to use his own later comment on Achilles—'cannot outfly our apprehensions' (II.iii. 110–11). Having likened human 'disasters' to the familiar knots that grow in pines, he continues reassuringly:

> Nor, princes, is it matter new to us
> That we come short of our suppose so far
> That after seven years' siege yet Troy walls stand;

Sith every action that hath gone before,
Whereof we have record, trial did draw
Bias and thwart, not answering the aim,
And that unbodied figure of the thought
That gave't surmised shape. Why then, you princes,
Do you with cheeks abash'd behold our works
And call them shames, which are, indeed, nought else
But the protractive trials of great Jove
To find persistive constancy in men,
The fineness of which metal is not found
In fortune's love? For then the bold and coward,
The wise and fool, the artist and unread,
The hard and soft, seem all affin'd and kin.
But in the wind and tempest of her frown
Distinction, with a broad and powerful fan,
Puffing at all, winnows the light away;
And what hath mass or matter by itself
Lies rich in virtue and unmingled.

                                        (I.iii. 10–30)

Agamemnon's phlegmatic trust that Jove in his own good time will end these 'trials' satisfactorily contrasts sharply with the nervy doubting Troilus at the play's beginning, who protested 'O gods, how do you plague me!' and fervently sought Apollo's aid. Where things 'ungain'd' had made the young man anxious and downcast, and things gained in Act III make him dream of a 'winnowed purity in love' which he fears may be unattainable—'How were I then uplifted!'—Agamemnon is only too ready to be uplifted by his easeful notion of the winnowing wind. (Keats, as may be guessed from the poems, was much moved by Troilus' blended joy and yearning and fear—'Death, I fear me,/Swooning destruction; or some joy too fine,/Too subtle-potent ...'—which he marked in his copy of the play). For in vaguely fancying that 'Distinction' like the wind will naturally puff the chaff from the grain, Agamemnon conveniently eliminates any need for human evaluative

judgement at all. By regarding the business as a mere matter
of meteorology he makes quite 'needless' any bother on
their own part of distinguishing sick from sound, or—as he
puts it—'hard and soft', 'bold and coward', 'wise and fool',
and so forth. His sedate exposition so smoothly balances
these opposites that it loses or blurs the distinctions
between them, as if to his mind they are really much of a
muchness no matter what the weather, or—in Pandarus'
dismissively levelling phrase—'all one to me'.

But the mind of the dramatist creating Agamemnon and
the rest of them is clearly very interested indeed in such
distinctions between 'hard and soft', 'wise and fool', and so
on, and in the distinctions (and affinities) between the
various ways these various people draw them and ignore
them and set store by them. Ulysses, for instance, unlike
Agamemnon does not so simple-mindedly assume that all is
well enough and that if it isn't, the broad and powerful fan of
'Distinction' will soon sort everything out. He diagnoses
their predicament very differently, and far from being
sanguine about future prospects, he fears that things are
bound to go from bad to worse unless the generals *do*
something to stop the rot at once. Troilus at the play's
beginning had wanly declared himself to be 'weak' in
contrast to the Greeks, who 'are strong, and skilful to their
strength'; but Ulysses in the council urges the Greeks to
grasp the vexing truth that Troy is still standing not because
of 'her strength' but because of 'our weakness'. He analyses
this weakness at considerable length, and his speeches seem
all the more cogent by contrast with the windiness of those
that came before. The dramatic structuring of the scene is
important, as always. For Ulysses does not reply
immediately to Agamemnon's speech (though his face and
demeanour may give some sign of what he is thinking);
instead, silver-bearded Nestor seizes the chance to
'apply/Thy latest words'—'With due observance of thy
godlike seat'—by rehearsing some favourite commonplaces
which endorse Agamemnon's view that all will soon be well.

Nestor's 'application' goes off at a slight tangent, but he too makes play with the notion that foul weather can be counted on to sort the strong from the weak; and buoyed up on the swell of his rhetoric he burbles on about bauble boats and strong-ribbed barks while Agamemnon benignly nods and thinks it rich (but happily not so rich as his own superior discourse which inspired it). It is hardly a wonder that Ulysses sees that the best way to puncture these flattering conceits and make these ostrich Greeks pull their heads from the sand and look about them, is by humouring 'mighty' Agamemnon and 'venerable' Nestor with elaborate obeisances and then contradicting what they have said while seeming merely to continue the discussion they have so wisely begun.

Ulysses' famous account of what is wrong hinges on his idea of the terrible chaos that follows when custom is invaded by anarchy, when order and degree are unsettled, confounded and then obliterated by riotous appetite. His initial commonplace images of cosmic orderliness give way to images of a universe horrifically awry:

> But when the planets
> In evil mixture to disorder wander,
> What plagues and what portents, what mutiny,
> What raging of the sea, shaking of earth,
> Commotion in the winds! Frights, changes, horrors,
> Divert and crack, rend and deracinate,
> The unity and married calm of states
> Quite from their fixture!
>
> (I.iii. 94–101)

This idea of everything being torn up by the roots sounds very frightful, and all the more so by contrast not just with Nestor and Agamemnon's soothing fantasies of natural disasters happening to unspecified others rather than the Greeks themselves, but also by contrast with the frivolous banter between Cressida and Pandarus in the previous

scene—for their mirthful trivia had seemed completely to
hedge out any thought of such possible enormities as these.
But these contrasts also accentuate both the extremity and
the generality of Ulysses' images, and so raise questions
about whether and how and why they are appropriate to the
current state of affairs in the Greeks' camp. Why does
Ulysses and only Ulysses speak of such things? It little avails
the audience at this point to know that this exposition
incorporates many ideas well known to Elizabethan and
Jacobean readers from such works as Elyot's *Boke named the
Governour* (1531). For, to apply Ulysses' own later words, we
'do not strain at the position—/It is familiar—but at the
author's drift'; and we strain still more to catch
Shakespeare's drift as Ulysses' speech continues, depicting
a world in which all distinctions are not just lost but
annihilated by 'appetite', which, when it has destroyed all,
must at last devour itself:

> Take but degree away, untune that string,
> And hark what discord follows! Each thing meets
> In mere oppugnancy; the bounded waters
> Should lift their bosoms higher than the shores,
> And make a sop of all this solid globe;
> Strength should be lord of imbecility,
> And the rude son should strike his father dead;
> Force should be right; or, rather, right and wrong—
> Between whose endless jar justice resides—
> Should lose their names, and so should justice too.
> Then everything includes itself in power,
> Power into will, will into appetite;
> And appetite, an universal wolf,
> So doubly seconded with will and power,
> Must make perforce an universal prey,
> And last eat up himself.
>
> (I.iii. 109–24)

This is the first occasion in the play (and by no means the

last, as it turns out) when an image of absolute chaos is invoked so as to cast a pall over the prevailing mood of wishfulness, and (partly for that reason) is thereupon disregarded by most of its hearers on stage. For the hearers in the audience, however, Ulysses' speech brings into the play an idea too sombre to be lightly set aside, though at this stage the likelihood of such an apocalypse seems remote, and it is not until the last Act that the destructive potential of lawless 'appetite' is borne in on us.

Not until he has conjured up this idea of total chaos does Ulysses clearly indicate its relevance to the Greeks' own case, with their enterprise wrecked by recalcitrance and insubordination, the whole army debilitated by 'an envious fever/Of pale and bloodless emulation.' Their consumptive disease thus grimly diagnosed by Ulysses sounds not merely inveterate but terminal—which makes the others' unruffled responses here seem all the more absurdly inappropriate. Nestor compliments Ulysses on his wisdom, and Agamemnon, showing no interest in the fever, calmly asks to hear the cure: 'The nature of the sickness found, Ulysses,/What is the remedy?' Instead of answering—or *as* his answer—Ulysses carries on with his detailed account of the malady, and in terms which cast an odd light back on all he has said so far, and an even odder light forward on what occurs later in the scene. For what we hear is less a matter of cool political analysis than a crescendo of righteous indignation directed at Achilles, who, it appears, is behaving with slanderous irreverence, loafing on his bed and roaring with laughter while his friends mimic both the high and mighty Agamemnon, 'in whom the tempers and the minds of all/*Should be shut up*' (as Ulysses had said earlier), and also Nestor, who 'should ... knit all the Greekish ears/To his experienc'd tongue'. Instead of being 'shut up' and obediently 'knit' to wisdom as they 'should', Achilles and his crew are scoffing at the great ones' authority and self-importance (including Ulysses' own, one suspects, though he neglects to mention this particular source of his vexation). In reporting these activities to his by now long-faced colleagues, Ulysses does not even momentarily see the funny side (only Diomedes' face perhaps shows the faint trace of a derisive grin), nor does he see how the jest is amplified by his own resentful humourlessness. He plays on Agamemnon's and Nestor's self-esteem as a way of pluming his own, but the rising tones of pique in his voice betray how he thinks it preposterous that anyone should make light of the weighty matter of 'our joint and several dignities' (to use Hector's later phrase). But if this is all that the appalling 'mutiny' and disruptive 'commotion' he warned of earlier amounts to—a lot of laziness, burlesque sport and scurril jests—then one discerns a rather exaggerative, reactionary and totalitarian streak in the analyst who is unable clearly to distinguish irreverent pranks from 'evil', sacrilege, the unleashed violence of voracious appetites. (The extremity of his earlier diagnosis now seems to have had behind it more than a touch of rigid absoluteness and repressive hysteria, rather like Angelo's in *Measure for Measure*.) What so exasperates Ulysses is that Achilles and his cronies debase all he stands for, and they can't be compelled to accept his valuations: in fact they are so unreasonable that they even mock wisdom, rationality and prescience—everything Ulysses values—and call these things by other degrading names. Like Thersites, Ulysses prides himself on his braininess and despises idiots like Ajax and Achilles the battering ram. But how can the 'intellectual' combat their derisory anti-intellectualism?

As Ulysses gets increasingly worked up about this uncontrollable unruliness, Nestor joins him in a duet of high-pitched moral indignation until the sudden arrival of Aeneas from Troy bearing Hector's challenge breaks into the council-meeting, and rather upsets the laden applecart of theory about 'degree' and hierarchy by not being able to tell which of these unvizarded faces belongs to the 'king of men', Agamemnon: 'How may/A stranger to those most imperial looks/Know them from eyes of other mortals?'. Like many of the non-recognitions and misrecognitions which stud the play, this one is highly comic, very like that in *Twelfth Night* when Viola begins her ambassadorial part by demanding, 'The honourable lady of the house, which is she?'—I.v. 158ff. And it is only the more comic because Agamemnon, though now alert to the chance of irony, is so unmajestically at a loss to tell if Aeneas is scorning him or being deferential.

The proclamation of Hector's challenge fortuitously sparks off Ulysses' brainwave about how to control the Achilles nuisance by using Achilles' overweening pride to bring about his fall. Contrary to Ulysses' previous view, that the fever raging among the Greeks carried 'death-tokens' and signs of 'no recovery' (to use his own later words), he now seizes on the notion that what Agamemnon patly called 'the remedy' is easily at hand: a few dollops of 'derision med'cinable' will soon physick the great Myrmidon and make him keen to serve again, obedient in his country's cause. But as we hear Ulysses outlining his plan to exploit and exacerbate the prideful emulation he had earlier deplored, we observe the large hiatus between his previous preaching and his actual practice, and realise that, like those of all the other characters in this scene and indeed throughout the play, every one of Ulysses' ample propositions is called into question by being dramatically juxtaposed with quite contrary views and perspectives, including his own elsewhere. The juxtapositions work not to cancel one thing with another but to make us question everything, see it from several angles at once. While Ulysses on occasion speaks more wisely than his associates do, this clearly does not mean that he is the play's spokesman, nor that the words of those who appear more stupid are therefore dramatically negligible, mere chaff as distinct from true grain. Ulysses' 'wisdom' and his 'design' are part of Shakespeare's dramatic design, but not the whole of it, and the effect of the whole is to cast a critical perspective on both—and the same sort of queering queries are raised about the sayings and 'designs' of all the others as well.

Every statement or suggestion made by every one of the characters is illuminated, qualified, questioned and destabilised by other things expressed in the drama elsewhere.

(iii)

It is clear throughout its first half that the play's centre of gravity lies close to its centre of levity. Gravely important matters are at stake even in all the lightness—the lovers' happiness, the fates of the two great rival nations. And while the early scenes are full of serious and heavy 'burden', they are at the same time 'passing full of the palm comical'. In so praising Shakespeare's great 'dexterity and power of wit', the 'never writer' had compared *Troilus* to 'the best comedy in Terence or Plautus', claiming also that the play (like Falstaff) is not only witty in itself but the cause of wit in others:

> And all such dull and heavy-witted worldlings, as were never capable of the wit of a comedy, coming by report of them to [Shakespeare's] representations, have found that wit there that they never found in themselves, and have parted better witted than they came, feeling an edge of wit set upon them, more than ever they dreamed they had brain to grind it on.

Whatever one makes of the cock-of-the-walk arrogance of this—its ascription of all dullness to 'they' and 'them'—the point surely applies to those who think their wits razor-sharp already, no less than to those who come blunt-witted and depart surprisingly honed by the play.

But how can this be? What sort of 'wit' is at work in *Troilus*, and how does it set an edge on ours? As soon as one starts to try to describe the kind of wit that is operating in the two scenes just considered, for example—the scene of

Troilus' giddiness and the Greek council scene—it is clear
that a rather complex definition is needed, to include not
only the great variety of humorous aspects but all the other
aspects that are bound up with those. The drama as we
experience it in these scenes is not a 'winnowed purity' of
either mirth or seriousness, 'unmingled'. Rather, it is a rich
and strange 'commixtion', in which the pleasing and
amusing elements are inseparable from the more
perturbing, painful and pitiful ones: it both is and is not
comical—just as, later on, it both is and is not tragical. In
short, we are dealing with a mongrel here—'mungrell tragi-
comedie'—which is perplexing, with no apparent 'rule in
unity'. Perhaps there is some sort of rule in *dis*unity,
disjunction? What sort of dramatic intelligence is this?

Of the definitions that come to mind none better fits the
case than Eliot's classic description of Marvell's wit:
listening to Troilus' rapture, we vicariously experience his
sense of imaginary relish of the coming sweetness, but at the
same time the poetry he speaks prompts in us 'a recognition,
implicit in the expression of [this] experience, of other kinds
of experience which are possible'—the possibility of love's
taste being 'mingled' instead of 'thrice-repured', of its being
perhaps distasted with the salt of broken tears, even the
possibility of its being not 'sweet' but bitter, gall. *His*
awareness is unsuspecting, concentrated, pure, single-
minded; and partly because his is so, ours is mixed,
multivalent. His sense and ours are incongruous, and in our
experience of the incongruity lies both the pathos and the
comedy of the scene. To us, the taste of this moment is
bitter-sweet. And that ever-varying taste of the multiplicity
of experience is the savour of the play's wit all through.

It is carried, often unbeknownst to them—as with Troilus
here—as a sort of latent charge in the characters' own
words. From the beginning, for example, the poetry
expressing Troilus' anxious hopes of joy has been charged
with suggestions of calamity and woe, the possibility of his
burning his lips, of his hopes lying drowned, of love

inflicting 'gashes' that no 'oil and balm' can soothe. But our
sense of him and of his chances in love is also partly shaped
by the associative suggestions carried in the language spoken
by others in other contexts. In the Greek council, for
example, when discussing the 'fever' in the camp, Ulysses
asks, 'When that the general is not like the hive,/To whom
the foragers shall all repair,/*What honey is expected?*' (I.iii.
81–3, my italics); and his question lodges obscurely in the
mind to be stirred again as we hear Troilus, with his
feverous pulse, panting in expectation of nectar and
sweetness. So too do the words of King Priam, for instance,
in the Trojan council scene, who says to his other lovesick
son, 'Paris, you speak/Like one besotted on your sweet
delights./You have the honey still, but these the gall ...' (II.ii.
142–4). Throughout the play, both in scenes where Troilus
is present and when he is not, the fair Cressida is always
being linked with this sweet Helen so bitter to her
countrymen, who brings such woe to Troy. Pandarus starts
this in the very first scene; in fact, he so closely associates the
two women that in Act III he implies that to his mind they
are virtually indistinguishable. He does so in the scene
immediately   before   the   scene   of   Troilus'   giddy
enchantment, when Pandarus and Paris and the 'enchanting'
Helen while away an idle hour in the exotic hothouse bower
of bliss where Paris cultivates his 'lily bed'. That scene of
erotic frivolity provides the context in which we next listen
to the besotted Troilus inviting Pandarus to 'fly with me to
Cressid' on Cupid's 'painted wings', and then ecstatically
taking off on his solo flight of fancy into the stratosphere of
ideal love, while his down-to-earth friend gets down to
business with his own kind of 'imaginary relish': 'I'll bring
her straight'.

    The dramatic placing of this scene of the lovers' meeting
not only highlights this contrast between the ardent
dreaming Troilus and the ribald expert Pandarus, but also
prominently contrasts each of these with Cressida's sense of
the occasion, which has an edge of each and yet is not

identical with either. Their various ways of experiencing this moment—Troilus', Pandarus', Cressida's own—are quite distinct, and mutually incompatible, yet none can be ignored, for they are all part of the watching audience's sense of this moment—and in our consciousness of them all at once, they clash, jolt, collide. This happens repeatedly in the play as we witness a conflict of views, and often the clash is violent, as in the betrayal scene in Act V, or indeed all of the scenes in which Thersites takes part. But even in scenes where discrepant experiences are not directly represented on stage, the drama set going in the audience's mind is always a conflict between disparate, co-present possibilities of experience. At every point we must somehow accommodate several distinct, incongruous and even incompatible ideas of what is happening.

This is the 'edge of wit' the drama sets on us—this sense of things clashing or grating or grinding against each other in our minds. Dr Johnson's famous phrase about heterogeneous ideas being 'yoked by violence together' in the wit of the Metaphysical poets is very apposite here, because the hostility between the disparate ideas or experiences—their mutual animus—does not dissolve into a synthesis or resolve into a comfortable ironic poise, or equilibrium, or ambiguity. It is not a case of opposite and discordant qualities being balanced or reconciled in our minds, for they remain discordant, antithetic and antipathetic, and the drama consists in the seemingly 'endless jarring' between them. Ulysses in the council, we recall, spoke with horror of the distinctionless chaos that would come if 'right and wrong—/Between whose endless jar justice resides—/Should lose their names ...'. His word 'resides', or (as spelt in Quarto and Folio) 'recides', is a textual crux on which various modern editors take different stands (cf., e.g., Riverside, Arden, Oxford). The Arden's gloss is that justice 'resides' in the opposition (the endless jarring) between what different people think right and wrong, that is, it derives from their contest. If this is accepted, this image of ceaseless disagreement which is *productive*—in this case, of justice—can also be seen as an apt image of how the play's own 'wit' works by producing its meanings out of opposition and quarrel. Its 'jarring' sometimes involves experiencing a direct contradiction of the type which Cressida pertly describes in the second scene—*'to say the truth, true and not true'* (my italics)—which takes its most extreme form in Troilus' bitterest moment of truth: 'This is, and is not, Cressid'. But more frequently the jarring or conflict is less headlong, more oblique—an abrasion, chafing, things fretting or rubbing against each other in our minds—and here again the play includes a predictive image of this, in the opening scene between Pandarus and Troilus: *'I speak no more than truth'*; *'Thou dost not speak so much'* (my italics).

This characteristic wit of the play, in which 'true' incessantly confronts 'not true', and 'no more than truth' rubs against 'not so much', marks *Troilus* as very much (like *Hamlet*) a play from the turn of the seventeenth century—a product of that immensely fertile, intellectually venturous and innovative time—however timelessly 'for all time' we may also judge it to be. This sort of wit, which was then much in vogue, is partly a way of exulting in and pondering an idea that was rather new and exciting at that time when so many of the old certainties and assumptions were being called in doubt by 'new philosophy', as Donne famously said—the idea that values are related to consciousness, and that consciousness is relative and variable, not absolute and uniform. At its best, such 'wit' is a means both of apprehending and analysing the sheer multiplicity and plenitude of human experience, and a means of exploring the relationships between distinct, diverse aspects or conceptions of reality, and of exploring their relative truth and value. In as much as the wit of *Troilus* is 'comprehensive' and explorative in these ways it cuts a lot deeper than the contemporary 'never writer' suggests. In fact, the terms in which he praises it prove quite inadequate, the more so as the play proceeds. For in commending the play to the relish of consciously superior intellectuals as distinct from less well-endowed 'worldlings', his terms imply only the rather manic, self-titillating type of wittiness to be found for instance in some of the smart young Jack Donne's elegies— 'The Perfume', say: an exultant but slightly frenetic wit, tickled and excited by its consciousness of its own skittish cleverness. But the wit at work in *Troilus* is not limited in this way. It is neither superficial nor evaporative. Nor is it content to dwell in anti-conventional brilliance, or riddling abstractions. It is much more searching than this, a new way of discovering and knowing the multifariousness of experience, not a species of knowingness. Indeed, to note a point I want to come back to, the play includes a profound critique of various kinds of knowingness.

Troilus contains many images suggestive of its peculiar edgy wit. One of these, already referred to, is especially germane here: Agamemnon's image of the 'conflux of meeting sap' whereby 'knots' are formed 'in the veins'. The play's dynamic wit is like a kind of conflux in which 'true, and not true' or 'is, and is not' are brought into conjunction, made to converge and merge with one another, and at the same time (in Troilus' later term) to 'co-act'. And the 'push and enmity' between them—the quarrel they excite—takes the form of that knottiest of questions, the nature of value. This particular philosophical and experiential knot recurrently marks the grain of the play throughout its course of growth. Ulysses says darkly that 'Blunt wedges rive hard knots'; and indeed the hard knotty issue of value, as the play conceives it, is very different from the sort of conundrum which in *Twelfth Night*, for instance, Viola trusts that time will 'untangle' for her because 'it is too hard a knot for me t'untie'. There is no untying this one. It can only be rudely split apart—or lived with, in all its funny and not funny problematical knottiness.

(iv)

Anyone familiar with commentaries on the play, who knows that its questioning of 'value' comes to a head in the analytical debate in the Trojan council scene, is likely to expect this to clarify the matter. The debate does not however sort everything out. This is not because the play is philosophically confused or (in Hector's words) 'unfit' or 'superficial', but because it is dramatising some specific (as distinct from purely theoretical) complexities involved in acts of valuing, and exploring the quarrels and contradictions that stem from these. The scene—like others throughout the play—includes much explicit discussion of 'value', 'worth' and so on, including some long passages of abstract analysis of a kind unusual in Shakespeare's plays, except around this period (though it is common enough in the works of contemporary dramatists such as Marston, Chapman, Beaumont and Fletcher). But as always in Shakespeare, the drama remains highly particular and concrete even when the characters' language is not. If extracted from its context, much of the argumentation here seems tortuous, recondite, intellectually formidable; but to an audience attending to the particulars of what is going on it is a fully integrated aspect of the scene. For what is going on is that a number of different people are trying to reach some agreed value-judgement of the situation they are in. The Trojans here not only discuss the concept of 'value' in the abstract, they are all the while engaged in the activity of valuing, estimating, prizing, weighing one thing in relation to another—as they (and all the others) have been doing since the start.

The specific item on their agenda—the question of whether to keep Helen and continue the war or send her back and end it—hinges on the question (as Troilus puts it), 'Is she worth keeping?'. Hector answers negatively, arguing that 'she is not worth what she doth cost/The keeping'—indeed, that she's not even worth the merest fraction of the cost in Trojan lives (each life as 'dear' as hers) spent in her defence. Troilus, repudiating this view, insists that the 'worth' in question cannot be measured in a 'scale/Of common ounces', nor (being 'fathomless') can it be plumbed, nor circumscribed by 'spans and inches so diminutive/As fears and reasons'. Hector and his brother Helenus are wrong to drag paltry 'fears' and 'reasons' into the issue, for the issue (as he sees it) is not just a question of the 'worth' of Helen in herself but the immeasurable worth attached to her or associated with her, of which she is as it were the symbol—'the worth and honour' of King Priam, no less, and by implication Troy's own 'worth and honour'. In ridiculing and rejecting his older brother's line of 'reasoning', Troilus moves the debate from particulars to general issues, raising the question of whether value is subjective or objective (i.e. whether value is ascribed by the valuer or whether it inheres in the object valued, or both). Here again no resolution to the quarrel is reached, for the brothers continue to see the matter very differently, with Troilus espousing the former theory ('What's aught but as 'tis valued?' he demands, with the air of a man vanquishing all opposition), while Hector insists, on the contrary, that value is not merely ascribed, not purely subjective, but inheres in the object as well:

> But value dwells not in particular will:
> It holds his estimate and dignity
> As well wherein 'tis precious of itself
> As in the prizer.
>
> (II.ii. 53–6)

This idea that value includes an objective element *as well as* a subjective element seems unexceptionable enough, though Hector merely asserts it to be so, without explaining how this bears on the case in hand. But Troilus immediately takes exception to it, pushes it aside, and continues to make out his case for keeping Helen by adducing a mish-mash of arguments-by-analogy—several of them grossly if unwittingly insulting to Helen (e.g. the idea of soiled silks, discarded left-over food, trade, etc). His gist is that, since the Trojans originally judged Helen to be worth stealing, she must be worth keeping, and that they cannot now reverse their earlier decision: 'there can be no evasion/To blench from this and to stand firm by honour'. In arguing this at some length Troilus appears to suppose that he is endorsing his own position on the subjectivity of value and contradicting Hector's, but in context his speech has something of the opposite effect, partly because it is riddled with self-contradictions and non-sequiturs and partly because of the way it clashes with other valuations expressed here and elsewhere, including the one which next follows it. For no sooner does Troilus end his speech with a stirring denunciation of Trojans who 'in [their] native place' 'fear to keep' the Helen they stole, than Cassandra enters, crying aloud her fear that their native place will be destroyed if they do keep what they stole: 'Troy burns, or else let Helen go'; and far from granting that this view of the situation has equivalent truth-value to his own ('What's aught but as 'tis valued?'), Troilus decides that it is nonsense, madly out of touch with reality.

According to Troilus, then, all valuations are purely subjective, but some (like Cassandra's) are more purely subjective than others (like his) and so can be ruled out of account, treated as insane. This reaction to his sister's intrusion into the debate starkly highlights Troilus' inconsistencies and exposes the contradictions between his theory of value and his actual practice. If (as he claims) value is simply ascribed by the valuer, then Helen for instance— or Cressida, indeed—simply 'is' what anyone cares to think her. But Troilus flatly denies this, insisting that his own valuations are correct and true, not merely for him but objectively true, no mere projection of his 'particular will' or figment of his fancy: his 'estimation' of Helen's worth is the one all right-thinking Trojans must accept and act on, and those who don't are wrong. In revealing this mismatch between theory and practice (which Troilus himself is unconscious of—just as he neglects the flat contradiction between his espousal of Helen here and his view of the matter in the opening scene), the drama here implicitly suggests that Hector's more complex idea of value is the more cogent. At the same time it clearly shows why this none the less leaves all particular questions of value wide open to dispute.

For if value 'holds [its] estimate.../As well wherein tis precious of itself/As in the prizer', how can these component parts—'objective' and 'subjective'—be separated and distinguished from each other so that people can agree about which is which and thereby agree about the true value of whatever is in question? The trouble of course is that the contents of each term are neither fixed nor absolute: they are relative terms, whose meaning in each case is therefore dependent on the meaning of the other. Only a blunt wedge can split the knot of subjective/objective value. And to complicate matters further, it is obvious that different 'prizers' have different conceptions of what constitutes each, so that what one person insists is 'objectively' the case, another hotly disputes, declaring it to be a mere projection of the 'prizer's' particular will. Whether or not values are considered inherent, the problem remains (as Ulysses later points out in his speech about time: III.iii. (145ff) that the human mind has no *reliable* and indisputable means of assessing them. Hector, later in the debate, tells Paris and Troilus that

The reasons you allege do more conduce
To the hot passion of distemp'red blood
Than to make up a free determination
'Twixt right and wrong....

(II.ii. 168–71)

But in this scene, as in previous and later ones, the drama

reveals very clearly to us, if not the characters themselves, why, even for the more cool-blooded among them, this business of 'making up' a 'free determination/'Twixt right and wrong' is hardly as straightforward as Hector's rather patronising and bland phrases here suggest. Indeed, his terms are reminiscent of those of Ulysses in the Greek council, when in the course of *his* classic conservative argument he used the more striking image of '*right and wrong,—/*Between whose endless jar justice resides', *losing their names* in a world taken over by what Hector here calls 'raging appetites' (I.iii. 116–8, italics mine).

In the Trojan council, then, as in many other scenes in the play, the drama turns precisely on the difficulty of making up a 'free determination' that people agree about instead of quarrelling over—the difficulty caused by the relativity (and hence radical unfixity) of subject and object, right and wrong, 'true and not true', wise and fool', 'bold and coward', worth and not worth, and so forth. (It is the relativity that renders all questions of 'value' in *Troilus* as highly contentious as the questions of 'justice' which occasion so much strife in *The Merchant of Venice*, say, or *Measure for Measure* or *King Lear*.) Our understanding of the issues here and of how much 'hangs upon [the] quarrel' is at once shaped and clarified by the drama of the preceding scenes, just as this scene in turn sheds light on those that follow. The princes' debate would have a different impact (and give the audience indigestion) if the play began with it, instead of beginning with scene after scene in which the characters continually gossip, fight, agonise and deliberate over particular questions about value, especially the 'value' or 'merit' or 'worth' (or worthlessness) of a particular person: Troilus, Cressida, Helen or Achilles or whoever.

One effect of all this disputation, in which every viewpoint expressed is dramatically countered or challenged by at least one and usually several others, is to excite *our* will to find or make a 'free determination' of our own, while making us realise how many contrary facts and values any such 'true judgment' would need somehow to encompass and comprehend. In presenting so many discrepant and competing valuations of everyone and everything, the drama itself is engaged in—and thereby embroils us in—a ceaseless activity of evaluative thinking which is analogous to the characters' own, yet which at the same time keeps us acutely aware of the relative and provisional status of *every* value-judgement, however absolutely expressed, and whether it is made by one or other of the characters or by ourselves as we watch. Hence, of course, all the critical quarrels.

'Oh Jupiter! there's no comparison', Cressida exclaims archly when Pandarus first declares that, between Troilus and Hector, 'Troilus is the better man of the two' (I.ii. 59). But Pandarus pursues the comparison ever more eagerly, flatly rebuffing her denial of his view with, 'No, Hector is not a better man than Troilus.... You have no judgment, niece'. Yet of course, as this scene makes so comically plain, 'judgment'—the capacity to estimate the value of anything—necessarily involves comparison and contrast (as every shopper in the market knows): the capacity to assess relative merit, to weigh one thing in relation to another, to observe fine distinction, gradation, degree. Pandarus knows this perfectly well when he tries to persuade his niece to share his favourable judgement of Troilus by adducing Helen's judgement in the matter—Helen 'prais'd his complexion above [that of] Paris'—which judgement Cressida effortlessly reduces to an absurdity. Troilus himself in the previous scene was far more susceptible to such persuasions:

Pandarus [If] her hair were not somewhat darker than Helen's—well, go to—there were no more comparison between the women. But, for my part, she is my kinswoman; I would not, as they term it, praise her, but I would somebody

Troilus   had heard her talk yesterday, as I did. I will not
                disprise your sister Cassandra's wit; but—
Troilus   O Pandarus!

                                          (I.i. 41–7)

—and off he goes in a transport of misery and ecstasy.
Throughout these early scenes we are thus prompted all the
time to think comparatively—to compare and contrast
Helen and Cressida, Hector and Troilus, Troilus and
Thersites, Pandarus and Ulysses, Ulysses and Agamemnon,
and so on.

Continually, our attention is drawn—via the characters'
judgements of themselves and each other—both to the
relative nature of particular valuations and to the large
'subjective' element of affective '*will*' in them, as when (for
Cressida's benefit, and ours) Pandarus does his running
commentary on who's who in the Trojan executive, as the
warlike brothers straggle home, each a trifle battered on
returning from the field. Never was a critical introduction so
laughably one-eyed. Perched 'up here'—'Here, here, here's
an excellent place; here we may see most bravely'—
Pandarus is in his element as compere of the royal
procession, quite beside himself with zeal to spot and hail
his favourite prince; so Cressida wittily grabs the chance to
hoodwink him completely:

Cressida   What sneaking fellow comes yonder?
           [*Troilus passes*]
Pandarus Where? yonder? That's Deiphobus. 'Tis
           Troilus. There's a man, niece. Hem! Brave
           Troilus, the prince of chivalry!

                             (I.ii. 218–21)

What you see and what you make of it has much to do
with what you *will*—as the sequel to this incident also makes
deliciously plain, when Cressida feigns keen interest in the
common soldiers who come next:

Cressida Here comes more.

Pandarus Asses, fools, dolts! chaff and bran, chaff and bran! porridge after meat! I could live and die in the eyes of Troilus. Ne'er look, ne'er look; the eagles are gone. Crows and daws, crows and daws! I had rather be such a man as Troilus than Agamemnon and all Greece.

Cressida There is amongst the Greeks Achilles, a better man than Troilus.

Pandarus Achilles? A drayman, a porter, a very camel!

Cressida Well, well.

Pandarus Well, well! Why, have you any discretion? Have you any eyes? Do you know what a man is?

(I.ii. 232–44)

Is Troilus a sneaking fellow or the prince of chivalry, or both? Helen, a priceless 'inestimable' pearl or a disastrous liability, or both? Is Agamemnon a 'king of men' or a nincompoop? Achilles 'a better man than Troilus' or 'a drayman, a porter, a very camel'? Achilles 'great' and 'valiant' or (as Ajax says) 'a whoreson dog'?

Ajax What is he more than another?

Agamemnon
  No more than what he thinks he is.

Ajax Is he so much? Do you not think he thinks himself a better man than I am?

(II.iii. 138–41)

Have you any discretion? Pandarus' question applies to us as well, as we try to weigh up all the competing claims; but if we begin by comfortably assuming that we are impartial adjudicators, exempt from the biases and fallibilities we see on every side, the scene between him and Cressida deftly dents that assurance by showing that an overview is no guarantee whatsoever of clear-seeing. The supposition that there is some ultimately sanctioned *right* and objective position is shown to be as wishful—and quarrel-provoking—as the (potentially frightening) idea that all values are purely subjective. And this applies with us as well as them. Like Queen Hecuba and Helen, we may as it were be stationed up in the 'eastern tower,/Whose height commands as subject all the vale,/To see the battle'; but to survey the scene with sovereign eye from this elevated vantage-point is not necessarily to avoid the subjectivities and controversies of those we watch. There is no infallible, god-like value-free position from which we, or anyone human, can view the action. *Every* perspective entails limits, and thus possible deficiencies of judgement. The drama anatomises and confronts us with this problem without providing any 'solution' or suggesting that any is possible.

The Trojans' council, like the Greeks', and like the other scenes surrounding these (and especially Ulysses' interview with Achilles in III.iii), confronts the characters and therefore us with another problem of valuation—that value-judgements, like everything else in this temporal world we live in, are always liable to change. Ulysses points out to Achilles that just as something may be 'dear in the esteem' and 'poor in worth', so something rich in worth may fall from favour, become 'abject in regard', undervalued or unvalued. What anyone thinks and feels at one moment is liable to be forgotten or contradicted or repudiated in the next. Troilus' question, 'why do you now/.../Beggar the estimation which you priz'd/Richer than sea and land?' (II.ii. 88–92) echoes again in many other scenes. The shocking reduction, stressed by the line-openings ('Beggar' what was 'Richer'), is like the one Achilles faces when (as Antony finds in *Antony and Cleopatra*) those who 'were us'd to bend,/To send their smiles before them to Achilles' now neglect him, for they 'bend' and 'turn' 'unplausive eyes' on him, treat him as a stranger or a nobody:

What, am I poor of late?
....
...they pass'd by me
As misers do by beggars—neither gave to me
Good word nor look. What, are my deeds forgot?
(III.iii. 74; 142–4)

The changeability of valuations which is a central issue in
Act III Scene iii and throughout the second half of the play is
foreshadowed many times in the early acts, and nowhere
more joltingly than when Hector in the council throws
caution to the wind, abandons all his previous arguments
against his brothers' desire to continue the war, and beams 'I
am yours'. The dangers attendant on the misvaluation of
danger-signs are not just academic.

(v)

The simultaneous recognition of multiple and discrepant
valuations which the play's wit sharpens in us is not
something that any of the characters shows much capacity
for. No one here has much of Hamlet's zany brilliance, say,
or a Falstaffian agility of imagination. Immersed in the
stagnancies and turbulence of their lives, in a world where
the brute facts of circumstance and of other people's wills
continually hamper or cut across their desires, they each
tend to assume that their own perspective on reality is more
accurate and more valid than anyone else's—indeed, in
many cases, the only conceivable one. In their different ways
they each incline to generalise their own experience, to 'steel
a strong opinion to themselves', to regard their own
valuations as absolutely right. And in view of the play's
wide-awake analysis of their tendency to forget or ignore
whatever may call in question the validity of their opinions,
it is perhaps surprising that so many critics are content to
equate the play's outlook with one or other of theirs.

Rather surprising, but not very: the need for definiteness, the desire to *settle* what's what, is as strong in watchers or readers of the play as it is in the Greeks and Trojans. For us as for them, complexities stimulate the need for simplicity, singleness. Chafed by doubts and contradictions, the mind tends to make the certainties it does not find. Dr Johnson in his *Preface to Shakespeare* (1765) remarked that 'the mind can only repose on the stability of truth', a comment that may strike our own more sceptical, relativistic age as having a rather quaintly eighteenth-century ring to it, so confident in its assumption that 'truth' is stably there in the world for the mind to rest on. But even though *Troilus* appeals to many modern readers largely because of its 'modernity'—its highly ironic consciousness of the instability of 'truth'—a lot of commentary on it in fact, whether wittingly or not, demonstrates the accuracy of Johnson's claim. The play designedly aggravates our need for surety. It makes such large demands on our imaginative and critical faculties—requiring us simultaneously to empathise in various ways with a great many different kinds of experience while also remaining critically detached—that it seems at once to arouse and frustrate our will to rest upon some stable truth amidst all the abrasive to-and-fro of disparate views. It draws us into concurrence with many of the characters' thoughts and feelings while constantly undercutting and contradicting every single ultimate 'truth' on which the mind might quietly repose. Many readers and audiences and producers have found the strain too much: the play is so full of frictions and unresolved conflicts that some find irresistible the temptation to flatten it into a neat pattern, to simplify what is so disturbingly multitudinous. Others feel impelled (again, like the characters) to fasten on to a supposed truth-source or a closed-circuit system of ideas which the play is thought to propound—even when this involves blocking out of consideration other elements which contravene or complicate or cast doubt upon this. Ulysses, traditionally a cunning fellow and shown in the play to have more nous than many, was for a long time the most popular candidate for this role of truth-sayer; new proponents each year still urge his merits as Shakespeare's spokesman. But for forty-odd years critics and producers have been more inclined to find in Thersites' views the nearest equivalent of the play's own, and to claim that it progressively draws us into agreement with him.

Troilus is by no means the only Shakespearian work whose readers have often supposed that its 'world view' is in large measure identical with the consciousness of one or other of the protagonists: *Othello*, seen either from Othello's perspective or from Iago's, was for many years a classic case, as was *Hamlet* and *King Lear*. But it seems to me as much a mistake in this case as with those, because here, as there, Shakespeare's myriad-minded wit is so significantly distinct from—and *not* reducible to—the kind of one-track unitary imagination that his created characters variously exhibit.

With *Troilus*, as with *Othello*, the supposition that the play's outlook matches that of one of its characters often involves neglecting or undervaluing its creative-critical intelligence. This is often the case in discussions or productions which regard Thersites' voice as the dominant voice of the play, and which naturally also conclude that the play itself is 'bitter' and 'negative'. Thersites, cursing the world, at one point exclaims, 'A plague of opinion! A man may wear it on both sides, like a leather jerkin'; and with him as with each of the others we surely need to inquire not just how far the play seems to endorse or share—and persuade us to share—his opinions, but also what it shows as the reverse side of the jerkin, so to speak, how far it establishes any limits or lacks in Thersites' outlook: is the play alive and intelligent in ways that he is not?

Similarly, a number of questions need to be thought about carefully whenever one encounters the related view—also widely held—that (as the Introduction to *Troilus* in the Riverside edition succinctly puts it), 'Despite its energy and

wit, the picture of man which it presents is pessimistic
almost to the point of nihilism'. Although a phrase like 'the
picture of man' is often used as a kind of shorthand, does it
not run the risk of misconstrual on several counts? To be
read aright, the singular, masculine 'man' must be
understood to mean 'mankind' and thus to include a
significant plurality of men *and* women, while 'the picture'
must be taken to mean something other and more
multifarious than the mere illustration of a single idea.
Again, does it make much sense to speak of 'the picture'
which the play presents '*despite* its energy and wit'?—as if the
very medium of the 'picture', and the energy of mind which
produces it, were ultimately extraneous; as if it could be set
aside, along with the poetry that embodies it, and the same
'picture' would still exist. Whether or not the play is judged
'pessimistic' (a lot of people prefer literature to be
'optimistic'), the more important question—as with any of
Shakespeare's great tragedies—is whether its sense of
human possibilities is compelling: does the drama convince
us that, yes, life can be like *this*? And once the play's
imaginative energy is properly recognised as an essential,
constitutive part of its attitude to life, does not the claim
that it borders on 'nihilism' begin to fall apart?

The basic point to keep hold of here is that the mind that
creates, directs and organises the drama in *Troilus* is
manifestly more comprehensive—sharper, deeper, more
magnanimous, above all more active and fertile—than that
of any of the characters, or indeed all of them put together.
Given the modern taste for irony (especially that of the
outsider, the malcontent) and the modern habit of regarding
such irony unironically, the play to some extent needs
rescuing from those who regard its critical spirit as
essentially (and praiseworthily) cynical or negative.
Cynicism is sentimentality in another mood, and neither of
these is the same as the play's searching, questioning
scepticism. The multiple ironies which arise in each scene
from the gaps between different characters' views and

between these and the play's larger sense of things are never merely reductive or circumscriptive in effect; indeed, to suppose that the *play* is reductive is itself a reductive misconstrual of how its sceptical attitude works dramatically, for one of its effects is precisely to explode the Mrs Slipslopian notion that all irony is a species of ironing that irons everything flat. The multiform ironic wit of *Troilus* is (to change the metaphors) a means not of narrowing but of complicating, broadening and deepening our perspective on the action, a way of pre-empting and challenging all single summary formulations of the significance of what we are shown.

Of course, the desire for summary formulations is strong, and there will always be people for whom Thersites sums everything up. Since all the grand ideals in the play are entangled with grand illusions, it is easy to suppose that the man who has the fewest illusions is the wisest man in a world of fools, the 'realist' who knows beyond doubt that human nature is thoroughly corrupt, thoroughly absurd. But beyond the question of how far we come to concur with Thersites' view of these lives and of life in general, and the question of how congenial we find *his* life—his being and his moral sensibility—is the question of how far his outlook represents and encompasses the play's, and all that the play brings us to notice and feel and realise as we watch.

To discern a good measure of truth in much of what Thersites says is no ground for taking it as the whole truth— any more than we do, for instance, in *King Lear*, when Goneril and Regan make some telling points about Lear's self-ignorance. When seen in the context of other things the play insist on but which he is insensitive to or unaware of, Thersites' scathing propositions often emerge as both 'true, and not true'—the assurances of a mind which prides itself on being unillusioned but which lacks discrimination, 'loses distinction' in its classificatory crudeness. Like Iago, Thersites is 'nothing if not critical', and therein lies both the force and the limit of his outlook. Partly because he lacks any capacity for doubt or wonder, he remains a man of restricted insight and imagination, devoid of human sympathy, lacking any sense of the possibility of tragedy, unable to take any critical perspective on his own minimalism—a person whose exultantly misanthropical cynicism expresses not a capacious intelligence but the shutting down of wit. Barking and snarling, Thersites spits out many a mordant home-truth. Yet (like everything else in the play) his reductive absoluteness—his habit of lumping everything into a few crude categories—is itself critically evaluated in relation to other kinds of thought and experience that are possible, for instance those of the ardent young maximalist Troilus, whose high aspirations soar beyond any dreamt of in Thersites' philosophy, or those of the play's other voluble *raissoneur*, Pandarus. Thersites' presence in the play is indeed of great importance, particularly in the last three Acts, and his indefatigable rasping energy has a vivifying and tonic effect, not just corrosive. But to equate his consciousness with the play's is to diminish the significance of each by 'losing distinction' between them, to flatten into a set of reductive 'propositions' what is an ample, open and dynamic play of *questions*—for that's the quarrel.

Rather than simply expressing a Thersitean view of love and war, the play scrutinises his particular way of being alive—as it does with all the others' ways as well. Thersites represents a basic and irreducible element in human nature as the play conceives it. His negatively reactive bent or disposition or mentality is perpetually on the offensive, armour-plated, and because it is pretty well unchangeable, it is also morally indestructible. This is one way—his way—of surviving in this world. (At the end, when Hector spares his life, Thersites' reaction to his escape is to curse Hector: 'a plague break thy neck for frighting me!' (V.iv. 30).) From first to last he is not much open to experience. Just as Troilus is incapable of being closed-off like Thersites, Thersites is incapable of experiencing the world or himself as Troilus does in III.i, for example: he is incapable of 'passion', of having anything *happen* to him or happen in him, incapable of ever being 'giddy', 'whirled', 'embraced' by longing or dread. To be humanly responsive to another person in the way Troilus is, for instance, is to be open to surprise, growth, change, pain, betrayal; but Thersites regards any such openness as sheer idiocy or lunacy. The play does not. Unlike him, it *is* capable of imagining and valuing the reality of 'such a passion' as Troilus', say, or Cassandra's dismay, or Achilles' rage when Patroclus is killed, and capable of awakening our imaginations to various possibilities of rapture and of anguish which Thersites can neither imagine nor comprehend. For us to be open to the drama involves being open (unlike Thersites) to the chance of something suddenly happening to *us*—the pain of the lovers' parting, for example, or the shock of Hector's death. Whereas the play is remarkable both for the vivid life it finds in callousness and callowness, *and* for the life it finds in sensitivity and susceptibility, Thersites is much more remarkable for the narrowness of his concerns. In contrast to the play's variableness—its many different kinds of degrees of comedy, its wide range of diverse tones, sounds and speech-rhythms—he varies little: his tones of voice and the kind of prose he speaks are much the same all through. Lost in the labyrinth of his fury, he has few other ways of relating to people, no perception of how his own nature partly creates the situation he ceaselessly protests against. Because his usual habit of mind is so acidly denunciatory, his invective, though often splendidly energetic, often seems compulsive, as if the effluent from a sewer is gushing forth out of control. His attacks lack some of the exhilaration of letting go, letting rip, which comes out for instance when Kent in *King Lear* (III.ii) abuses and beats up the 'lily-liver'd' Oswald—where Kent seems fully alive in his rage, partly because he is elsewhere capable of being *not* like this.

Before concluding that the play's sense of life is

commensurate with Thersites', therefore, it is as well to recall how they differ as well as what they have in common; for to do this is to see that while its spirit is partly Thersitean (the play would be very different and a lesser thing if he weren't in it), it also partakes something of all the others' various natures as well: something of Pandarus' bawdiness, Troilus' excitability, Cressida's drollery, Achilles' aggressive unamenability, and so forth—and yet, like the Ajax who 'hath robbed many beasts of their particular additions', the whole turns out to be much more than the sum of its parts.

With Thersites, then, as with all the others, the play gives considerable salience to his views while also casting a quizzical, inquisitive light on them; and a brief exchange at the end of Act III suggests one of the main terms of this dramatic inquiry: 'ignorance'. Earlier in the scene, Ulysses has upset Achilles by announcing that the latter's supposedly secret love-affair is public knowledge, for 'the providence that's in a watchful state' moves in mysterious ways and 'finds bottom in th' uncomprehensive deeps'; left to mull over all this Achilles frowningly mumbles,

> My mind is troubled, like a fountain stirr'd;
> And I myself see not the bottom of it.
> [*Exeunt Achilles and Patroclus*]

> Thersites Would the fountain of your mind were clear again, that I might water an ass at it. I had rather be a tick in a sheep than such a valiant ignorance.
>
> (III.iii. 303–8)

The immediate effect here is shrivellingly comic; and yet as we laugh we also realise that Thersites' scorn reveals something about him as well as about Achilles, for he cannot imagine being 'troubled' or mystified in Achilles' way. For him, all is clarity, 'surety secure', and he supposes he always sees to the bottom of everything. On other occasions in the play, we've heard various other characters declare what they would 'rather be', were they someone other than themselves (a turn of mind strangely common in many of Shakespeare's plays: 'were I anything but what I am,/I would wish me only he', as Coriolanus says of Aufidius, for example). Thersites himself later in the play says, 'Ask me not what I would be, if I were not Thersites; for I care not to be the louse of a lazar, so I were not Menelaus' (V.i. 59–60). His mind runs on bloodsuckers, and indeed his fancy that life as a tick in a sheep would be preferable to being 'such a valiant ignorance' itself gives us the notion that there is something ticklike, parasitical, in the way he feeds off the lives of the larger hosts he despises, curses, jeers at—as with Ajax: 'I would thou didst itch from head to foot and I had the scratching of thee; I would make thee the loathsomest scab in Greece' (II.i. 26–8). His conviction that he has a monopoly on wit is shown to be not entirely false, but that does not mean that the play endorses it. He is always scoffing at other people for being half-witted or (as he wittily says of Agamemnon) having 'not so much brain as ear-wax', and forever railing against the 'folly and ignorance' which he sees as 'the common curse of mankind'. But whether he is exempt from this condition is a question we are made to ponder. So is the question of whether *we* are. And so is the even more basic question of quite what the play (as distinct from Thersites) includes in the term 'ignorance' on this and all the other occasions where it is raised.

For one of the key distinctions we are pressed to think about as we consider the relative terms 'wise' and 'fool' is not between 'wit' and brainlessness but between 'wit' and 'ignorance'. If wit is (broadly speaking) intelligent awareness, including awareness of other possible ways of experiencing the world, then 'ignorance' is its obverse, and it takes many forms in the play, the most basic one being 'innocence', unknowingness—being uninformed (e.g. about what the future holds), or as we say, 'unwitting'. *All* the characters—like us watching them—are necessarily 'innocent' in some respects, including Thersites and Ulysses (despite 'the providence that's in a watchful state') and including the prophets Cassandra and Calchas, who claim that they have 'sight' in 'things to come'; and this innocence or obliviousness is one of the things the drama is mirthfully and sympathetically focused upon from first to last. But along with this, the play is exploring another dimension of 'ignorance', the capacity for *ignoring* things, ejecting them from the mind, which is variously termed 'ignorance', 'neglection', 'evasion', 'negligence', 'oblivion', 'forgetting'.

The characters' *ignoring*, like their ignorance, takes many forms, of which one is complacency (neglecting or being oblivious to other possible facts or ideas)—as in Agamemnon's or Ulysses' pontifical pronouncements, or Thersites' reductive cynicism, which, by assuming that he alone is plugged into the truth, shows a lack of wit about the possibility that he might not be. Another sort of ignoring or neglection is self-engrossment, such as Paris' or (more gigantically) Achilles', whom Ulysses memorably characterises as a 'proud lord/That bastes his arrogance with his own seam [fat]/And never suffers matter of the world/Enter his thoughts, save such as doth revolve/And ruminate himself...' (II.iii. 179–83). Then again, there is the 'ignorance' of concentrating exclusively on the 'extant moment', while 'what's past and what's to come is strew'd with husks/And formless ruin of oblivion' (IV.v. 166–7). Conversely, there is the ignoring of the current moment by concentrating exclusively on an idea of the past or a dream of what the future holds. There is also the kind of ignoring that Falstaff in *Henry IV, Part Two* both feigns and is afflicted by, the disease of not listening, the malady of not marking. The Hector who in the council chides his brothers on the grounds that 'pleasure and revenge/Have ears more deaf than adders to the voice/Of any true decision' is the man who in Act 5 himself appears (like Agamemnon) to have less brain than ear-wax: he is fatally deaf to the pleas of wife, sister and father, 'stop[s] his ears against admonishment'.

This 'ignoring'—this individual and collective deafness, blindness, heedlessness—the play dramatises and reflects upon in many forms, and its workings and consequences are the focus of much of our laughter, pity and dismay. In thus discerning the characters' relative lack of wit, we find in it the absurd, fearful and possible image of our own. In the latter half of the play it becomes progressively more fearful; but even in watching the drama of the first two Acts, 'there can be no evasion/To blench from this': such ignorance is everywhere. It is endemic among the Greeks, of course. But the most chronic cases of all come in the Trojan council after Hector reminds his brothers that 'modest doubt is call'd/The beacon of the wise, the tent [or probe] that searches/To th' bottom of the worst', and the debate is suddenly interrupted by someone searching to the bottom of the worst, when Cassandra's shrieks and cries pierce the air: 'Cry Trojans, cry./.../Let us pay betimes/A moiety of that mass of moan to come./.../Our firebrand brother, Paris, burns us all./.../...Troy burns, or else let Helen go.'

This has the effect, on us, of a terrible apparition. It is as if the ghost of the future has suddenly materialised, in the very instant when her brothers are electing this frightful destiny. With prophetic tears she weeps at events that are latent in the here and now, but because her vision doesn't match her brothers' dreams of 'promis'd glory', they all ignore it, deny its force, dismiss it as 'brainsick raptures'.

Watching the play, we, unlike them, cannot ignore this spectre of the sack of Troy. It enters into our experience, modifies our sensibility, becomes part of the very taste of every moment of what follows.

· 3 ·

'The monstruosity in love'

In contrast to *Romeo and Juliet* and *Antony and Cleopatra*, surprisingly few scenes in *Troilus and Cressida* are devoted directly to the love-affair between the title figures. Cressida appears in only six, while Troilus is with her and speaks with her in only four of these. Yet the title, with its bifold stress on relationship and separateness, points to the heart of the matter. The paralleling of the different plots and the 'corresponsive' concerns of each draw attention at every stage to the bearing of the war scenes on the love-affair, and vice versa. And at the centre, in Acts III and IV, Shakespeare presents a run of scenes which suddenly sharpen and deepen the emotional focus of the play—scenes in which Troilus and Cressida at last joyfully come together, only to be abruptly parted, bereft of each other by 'the chance of war'. Whereas the drama in Acts I and II has been predominantly detached, perspicacious, coolly analytic, here it reaches further inward into the interiors of the characters' experience, while continuing to cast everything in an ever more disquieting ironical light.

These scenes of the lovers' union and sudden separation when Cressida must go to the Greeks (III.ii to IV.iv, inclusive) are among the most powerful and memorable in the play, which means that their power is part of what makes the play so moving as a whole. In considering them both in themselves and in relation to their larger context it is worth recalling Chaucer's *Troilus and Criseyde*, which Shakespeare freely draws on and adapts to his own purposes here, in a manner that both assumes and exploits his audience's knowledge of Chaucer's narrative of 'the double [sorrow] of Troilus', and 'In lovynge, how his aventures fellen/Fro wo to wele, and after out of joie'. What one makes of the comparison between play and poem depends, of course, on what one makes of each independently; but setting them beside each other (as the play implicitly invites) can help in identifying their joint and several potencies—and in particular the play's own in its middle scenes. Here, as in the war scenes, Shakespeare's originality can be seen both in his uses of and departures from his source material—in what he takes and remakes anew, in what he omits, and what he adds. A great deal has been written about the play's relationship to the poem, most of it placing the main stress on their marked dissimilarities: the *contrast* between them, especially their differences in tone and temper, is generally thought more notable than what they have in common (beside the basic love plot, of course, and some aspects of characterisation). But it is worth noticing also that many of these differences derive from and underscore a deep imaginative affinity between the two works, which is evinced most clearly in the ways their central love scenes are conceived in relation to what precedes and follows.

Perhaps the main respect in which the play is (in Agamemnon's phrase) 'affin'd and kin' to the poem which partly inspired it, even while the two are also strikingly 'distinct', may be summed up in terms of some comments Chaucer's Pandare makes early on, when he seeks to encourage the love-lorn Troilus to take a larger view of things by reminding him that 'By [its] contrarie is every thyng declared'; and he elaborates by suggesting that the taste of 'swe[e]tnesse' cannot properly be known by anyone that 'nevere tasted bitternesse', since 'no man may ben inly glad, I trowe,/That nevere was in [sorrow] or som destresse':

Eke whit by blak, by shame ek worthinesse,
Ech set by other, more for other semeth ...

(Chaucer, *Troilus and Criseyde*, I. 637–8, *et seq.*)

Pandare's words provide a neat formulation of what, broadly speaking, can be seen as the operative principle of the poem itself, governing the way Chaucer conceives and organises his material: throughout the poem 'every thyng' is 'declared' (manifested, made known, shown forth) by its 'contrarie', and the reality and value of each—Troilus' joy and his sorrow, for example—are thus fully discovered and realised only in being thus 'set by other'. And as is clear from its opening on, and by no means least in its central scenes, the play too, in a much more radical and comprehensive way, is everywhere informed by an heuristic sense of contrariety which is expressed throughout in formal terms, moulding and shaping its every aspect: its dramatic language, its characterisation, its scenic design, its placing and ordering of scenes, and so forth—and thus shaping the whole sense of life which it expresses.

This is not to say, of course, that the play (any more than the poem) thinks of human experience in static terms of opposite extremes 'as gross/As black and white' (to use Henry's phrase in *Henry V*, II.ii. 103–4), nor that it sees everything as a simple case of either/or, whether 'shame' or 'worthinesse', 'passion' or 'reason', or what not—though many of the characters in it tend to do just that, and quite a few of its critics have followed suit. As in the poem, so in the play, the exploration of 'contraries' probes not merely their opposition or their complementarity but their inter-dependency as well, whereby each is seen as a potential form of the other. The finer intermediate shades and degrees of grey, so to speak, are of as much interest as the black and white at either end of the spectrum. At every point the drama works contrastively, setting things 'by other' so that they mutually accentuate and illuminate each other. Thus,

for example, in the play as in the poem, Troilus' 'wo' in Act
V is dramatised in relation to his brief experience of 'wele',
when 'Cressid is mine'—and vice versa; the contrary
experiences are interdependent, the meaning of each being
dramatically 'declared' 'by other'. The value of the lovers'
'unity' is realised by each of them—and, in another sense,
by the play itself—in terms of their previous and later
experience of division. And (no less significantly, though
the point is more easily missed) the same is true the other
way as well.

The middle scenes, like the previous ones, include a
variety of images and metaphors suggestive of the way the
play itself works here. One such comes at the end of Act III
when the extreme cynic Thersites (who is thus implicitly
contrasted with the extreme romantic Troilus) mocks the
idiot Ajax as one who

> bites his lip with a politic regard, as who should say
> 'There were wit in this head, an 'twould out'; and so there
> is; but it lies as coldly in him as fire in a flint, which will
> not show without knocking.

(III.iii. 254–8)

The image suggests something of how the play's own 'wit'
flashes out in these scenes as elsewhere, as the 'flint' is
'knocked' to 'show' the 'fire'. This 'knocking' or friction,
whereby sparks or flashes of meaning are struck out of
contrasts, is far more pronounced and incessant than
Chaucer's mode of 'declaration', and it makes for many of
the major differences between the two works—especially
the differences in pace and texture between the poem's love
scenes and the play's. Chaucer renders the little-by-little
unfolding of the lovers' relationship—detailing all their
fluctuant fears, desires, despairs and hesitant venturings
until Pandare's elaborate machinations eventually trick
them into bed, whereafter they share three years of loving
before Criseyde is sent to the Greek camp as she had

dreaded all along. Shakespeare foreshortens the time-span and contracts the whole drama of their love into a few momentous scenes so that the lovers come together for a single night, a single scene, before morning brings acute distress of a kind they had not envisaged at all.

The extreme compression of the play's love scenes has often been taken as evidence that Shakespeare's conception of love here is predominantly 'derisive', 'bitter', 'negative', as distinct from Chaucer's 'sympathetic', 'positive', 'affirmative' one. But to understand the principle of mutually declarative contrasts which governs the play's design is to see that such an account makes *Troilus* sound far more uniform, single-toned (monotonous), than it actually is. The play severely calls into question romantic conceptions of love and heroic conceptions of war, but it does not choke off its questions by propounding or driving home a rigidly anti-idealist view of either. Its sense of both is less cut-and-dried and less exclusively conclusive than such a view of it suggests, and its valuations of 'every thyng' include a large measure of sceptical intelligence even about what constitutes evaluative conclusiveness in these as in other moral matters.

This interrogative thrust of the drama, its intense *questioning* energy, can be felt at every turn and counter-turn in these central scenes. Here, as in Acts I and II, the play's vitality flares out of its contrasted possibilities of experience, its clashing perspectives, its swerves of angle, its sudden unreliable changes of key. So here as before it is 'needful' to set one's sense 'on the attentive bent', to notice how all these 'knockings' and juxtapositions work dramatically.

(i)

Another way to suggest how they work—for it is one form in which the tensions of the drama here make themselves felt—is in terms of a musical metaphor which the play repeatedly invokes, most famously in Ulysses' speech in the Greek council when he speaks of what happens when 'degree' is taken away: '...untune that string,/And hark what discord follows'. In the early Acts the sounds of human experience in love and war to which we must harken are for the most part 'untuned', discordant, and by the end of the play the din has become a horrible cacophony. But what makes the central love scenes so unforgettable is that here the lovers' hearts and voices come to be for the first time in tune with each other, and the long-awaited possibility of 'sweet music' between them is realised; and at the same time the play poignantly intimates its transience, its vulnerability to everything in the surrounding world and in the lovers themselves which may 'untune' or fray or even break the heartstrings of their love.

In expressing these opposed possibilities of music and discord, each of which is implicit in—a potential form of— the other, the play's own dramatic 'music' is here accordingly complex, sweet and bitter both at once, both in and out of tune. To catch its special quality one needs to heed the way each scene is 'set by other', and also, *within* each scene, to hark at how each speech, each phrase, each thought and feeling, each shade of tone, is 'set by other' so that they vibrate together—chime or jar—in the mind. This applies not only in the great scenes between Troilus and Cressida but also in the adjacent scenes; for instance, Act III Scene i, the remarkable scene between Paris and Pandarus and Helen, which also serves as the overture for this next phase of the play.

The shift from Act II to Act III is marked by a striking change of temper and tempo—of 'atmosphere', setting, pace, tone. Before, everything had seemed constrained by aggression or defensiveness of one sort or another, everyone boxed in by the exigencies of siege. But here there are refreshing signs of ease, accord, amity. A new sound is heard in the air. Since the play began, we have heard on and off the

'ungracious clamours' and 'rude sounds' of military alarms
and retreats—the noisome noise of brazen, strident
instruments of war. But now the sounds of sweeter
instruments waft abroad enticingly, the sounds of delighted
harmony, played for the 'pleasure' of those 'that love
music'. And this 'good broken music' (music 'in parts',
presumably played on instruments of different families, for
example woodwind and strings) at once suggests and
accompanies a like kind of agreeable 'music' in human
relationships. Instead of anxious love-pangs or
argumentative crossfire or the sound of fury, scorn-spiked
ridicule and all the 'performance of ... heaving spleens', the
encounter with which Act III Scene i begins is much more
equable, amicable: 'Friend, you—pray you, a word'. The
servant thus addressed by Pandarus takes his chance to play
the fool by making merry sport from the duplicity of
words—pretending (as Cressida had done in I.ii) not to
grasp what Pandarus is driving at. But whereas in the scene
(II.1) between Ajax and the fool Thersites, the latter's ploy
of incomprehension had excited only bare-fanged malignity
and brutish aggression—'Dog!'—here the chances of
division and misapprehension are lightly parried, kept
benign: 'Friend, we understand not one another: I am too
courtly, and thou art too cunning'. And this little dialogue
between Pandarus and the divergent-thinking servant,
couched thus in such terms as 'friend', 'depend', 'praise',
'faith', 'grace', 'honour', 'music', and the like, sets the tenor
of what follows when Helen and Paris enter, for Pandarus
continues in the same vein—'full of fair words'—as the
threesome harp together on the keynotes 'fair' and 'sweet',
speaking of 'fair desires' 'fair company', 'fair thoughts' 'fair
pillow', 'fair pleasure' 'sweet queen' 'honey-sweet lord', and
so on. All this sweetness soon seems cloying, or a saccharine
disguise for something more sour (the scene is sometimes
played with the lovers ganging up on Pandarus). But even
though the 'good broken music' has been interrupted by
Pandarus' coming—'you have broke it, cousin', puns

Paris—the breach is temporary and mendable, for he 'shall make it whole again' with a tune that pleases all. Any 'melancholy' here can be dissolved in 'melody' and mirth.

Coming after all those scenes fraught with the disputes and competitions of male egos (especially in the womanless and rancorous Greek camp), the seductive allure of this pampered world of pillows and music, teasing compliments and voluptuous idleness, provides a welcome change from so much animosity and frustration, the silly-sweet banter a lighter relief from high-flown intellections or foul-mouthed abuse. (If the trio's exchanges are played as nastier than this, of course the contrast is lost.) For in all this jesting and laughter which climaxes in Pandarus' song, the scene presents an image of possible congruence and reciprocity in human affairs which is the opposite of all that earlier strain and stress and 'quarrel'. The contrary of contrariety and conflict, so to speak, is momentarily imaged in this little interlude which is so 'full of harmony'.

Yet while this is part of the scene's effect, it is clearly not the whole, for over and against the seductive harmonies another kind of 'good broken music' is audible, to which Pandarus and the rest are oblivious, and which harshly grates against their 'sweet' sounds of civility and conviviality—a music made of the reverberations of all those previous scenes of stalemate and confrontation that constitute the ugly reality of the Trojan War, the fight over Helen. Although the second scene of Act I has afforded a passing glimpse of the face that launched a thousand ships, the structuring of the play has delayed any closer view of her until now when the Trojans are recommitted to defending her at whatever cost. 'Well may we fight for her whom we know well/The world's largest spaces cannot parallel'; 'she is a theme of honour and renown, /A spur to valiant and magnanimous deeds': the clash between those heady abstractions and fervid urgencies of the council debate and this scene's feather-brained cosy-nested trivialities is extreme; and it is all the more unsettling when amidst their raillery and heated ribaldries ('hot blood', 'hot thoughts', 'hot deeds') they speak of the war in tones and terms so sublimely self-unseeing ('I would fain have arm'd to-day, but my Nell would not have it so'), and seem so entirely undisturbed by the possibility which Helen casually mentions here, that 'this love will undo us all'. Cassandra's dissonant premonition of Troy's 'undoing' is converted now to melodious mirth as Pandarus sings at Helen's request, 'Love, love, nothing but love, still love, still more':

> Love, love, nothing but love, still love, still more!
>> For, oh, love's bow
>> Shoots buck and doe;
>> The shaft confounds
>> Not that it wounds,
> But tickles still the sore.
> These lovers cry, O ho, they die!
>> Yet that which seems the wound to kill
> Doth turn O ho! to ha! ha! he!
>> So dying love lives still.
> O ho! a while, but ha! ha! ha!
> O ho! groans out for ha! ha! ha!—hey ho!
>> *Helen* In love, i' faith, to the very tip of the nose.
>>   (III.i. 109–21)

The song epitomises the disturbing double-edged quality of the whole scene, in making us laugh and wince at the same time: its risqué jokes at once invoke and make light of the real risks of violence and death implicit in the hunt for love, and the chance of pain and desolation is shadowed behind the chance of delight which the ditty so exuberantly celebrates. Cassandra's cries, still echoing in our minds, serve as a piercing reminder that what this tittering trio take as such a supreme laughing matter is also potentially a weeping matter in which all the terms can have another meaning, and 'undo', 'confound', 'wound', 'cry', 'die', 'kill' and 'groans' can spell quite the opposite of 'ha! ha! ha!'.

Throughout the song and the scene as a whole the contrary
possibilities of experience thrown up by the dramatic
language knock against each other in this fashion, so that, far
from unambiguously imaging a world of 'love, nothing but
love', the scene continually sets that ideal of union and
security—imperfectly realised though it is—against the co-
present possibilities of loss, severance and war. Nowhere do
they clash more disturbingly than in the closing speeches,
after another brassy retreat blares out to signal the warriors'
return from battle, and Paris, who in the council had wooed
Hector to fight for Helen, now says caressingly and with
terrible unconscious irony,

> Sweet Helen, I must woo you
> To help unarm our Hector. His stubborn buckles,
> With these your white enchanting fingers touch'd,
> Shall more obey than to the edge of steel
> Or force of Greekish sinews.
>
> (III.i. 142–6)

There, for a fleeting moment (echoing other such
moments in the council—'a Grecian queen, whose youth
and freshness/Wrinkles Apollo's, and makes stale the
morning'—where her 'freshness' verily increases the
creasiness of Apollo's wrinkles), the subtle-potent allure of
Helen's beauty is marvellously realised in verse which sets
the living touch of her 'white enchanting fingers' over
against the deadly 'edge of steel'. The image of a peaceful
surrender, of Hector being 'helped' to unarm, his 'stubborn
buckles' obeying the touch of these delicate feminine hands,
is superimposed on an image of the hideous converse
possibility, which Paris' silky voice lights on only to
disarm—of Hector being powerless to resist the 'force' of
these Greekish swords and sinews. To notice this is to
notice how the irony here as throughout the scene serves not
to undercut but to complicate and intensify the drama's
emotional power. To harken to this 'broken music' is to be

moved to something much less comfortable than a wry
shrug of cynical amusement, aloof and detached. For if
crystal-voiced Helen's self-preening reply to Paris here at the
end of the scene confirms her moral vacuity and the
grotesque absurdity of the war, the prospect that her
dalliance with Paris may cost Hector's life and Troy's is not
thereby made any the less distressing, but rather more.

(ii)

All of the play's juxtapositions and contrasts are double-
edged like this—they cut both ways—which is why the
ironies they generate are never just deflationary and never
one-directional. (The play would be much easier to take if
they were.) And here a prime example is the scene change
from Act III Scene i to Scene ii.

Not the least disquieting effect of Act III Scene i is its
implied bearing on Troilus and Cressida, whose names are
on everyone's lips in tones of frisky knowingness as Troilus'
quest for privacy becomes a topic for public chortling,
salacious innuendo topped with the cream of camp jokes
('You'll remember her brother's excuse?' 'To a hair', quips
Paris, remembering Troilus' celebrated jest about 'the
forked one' (cf. I.ii. 130–60).) The mix-up at the scene's start
concerning 'the mortal Venus', which Pandarus takes as a
reference to Cressida when the servant actually means
Helen, reactivates the questions raised explicitly at the
play's beginning, as to whether (as Pandarus thinks) the two
women are as like as two peas, or whether (as Troilus thinks)
they are so distinct that 'there's no comparison', or whether,
as with so much else in the play, it isn't a matter of either/or
but (much more troublesomely) both/and—questions kept
open here by the persistent linking of Helen's and Cressida's
names, which of course also implies a parallel between Paris
and Troilus.

These questions recur with the change of scene to Act III

Scene ii—Troilus' and Cressida's meeting—for the contiguity of the two scenes works to compare and contrast the two couples. The scene begins as if in repeat performance of that between the previous threesome, with Pandarus again quizzing a servant as to the lovers' whereabouts. But this opening also differs from that of the earlier scene in its urgency, the lack of leisure for idle jests. And indeed, what follows confirms the differences in tenor and tone between this 'orchard' scene and that previous one set in the cosseted luxury of Paris and Helen's habitat—so much so that it is surprising to find a great many critics and stage-directors happy to follow Pandarus in treating the two pairs of lovers as if they were pretty well indistinguishable.

This way of reading the play, whereby Cressida and Helen in particular are both alike judged worthless from the outset, links with and is compounded by another common tendency (especially in readings that give great prominence to scenes such as the councils and those at the end), a tendency to down-play the more intimate love scenes in the middle (III.ii, IV.ii and IV.iv), rather as if these were merely steps on the way to the great scene of Cressida's infidelity in Act V. Since we are all presumed to know (from Chaucer and Henryson and from later versions of the story) that she proves faithless in the end, the central scene, on this account, can be viewed chiefly in the light of that terminal fact—Troilus being seen as rather a goose for loving someone so clearly not worth it, and Cressida's love of him being discounted as more or less nugatory because she later turns her attentions so speedily to Diomedes. Even in accounts or stage productions less absolute about the matter, one notices a tendency to read the ending back into the middle, to regard the ironies as purely reductive and hence to treat the ultimate outcome as determining the value (i.e. the worthlessness) of their love.

But while the strong sequential movement of the drama indeed makes the ending crucial, it is not (in my view) all-important, and not the sole determinant of value either in the love-affair or in the war. And in both connections, notwithstanding the manifold ironies of the Trojan council, a remark made there by Troilus is highly relevant: his point that 'we may not think the justness of each act/Such and no other than event doth form it'. For to think the value of this love or the war 'such *and no other* than event doth form it', is to suppose that the reality and value of the earlier scenes is in effect wholly defined by what follows in the final Act. But this distorts the drama by supposing that its ironies work simply to negate or undermine what in fact they serve powerfully to 'declare' and emphasise. For the play insists, conversely, that the value of the ending itself depends upon the value of what went before, and has meaning only in relation to and *in contrast to* those other very different actualities and possibilities of experience imaged in the previous scenes.

Here again, various exchanges within these middle scenes alert us to notice how the different aspects of the play are interrelated. For instance, there's the servant's banter with Pandarus, which pointedly opens Act III:

> *Pandarus* What music is this?
> *Servant*   I do but partly know, sir; it is music in parts.
> *Pandarus* Know you the musicians?
> *Servant*   Wholly sir.
>
> (III.i. 16–19)

And just as this draws attention to how the concurrent 'parts' or voices in this scene itself comprise a carefully composed 'whole', so it applies on a larger scale to the different parts of the whole play, as indeed the opening exchange here also tickles us to notice, via the servant's jokes about the significance of *sequence*—whether physical or temporal sequence, or a social or moral order of priority (this 'courtly' conversation harks back ironically to the previous talk about hierarchy and 'degree'):

Pandarus   Do you not follow the young Lord Paris?
Servant   Ay, sir, when he goes before me.
Pandarus   You depend upon him, I mean?
Servant   Sir, I do depend upon the lord.
Pandarus   You depend upon a notable gentleman; I must
           needs praise him.

(III.i. 1–7)

The different kinds of 'depending' to which the word-play draws attention all have their analogues in the play's internal design. Like the servant at the heels of his lord, what 'follows' or comes after this scene has its own vitality even though it also 'depends upon' and derives its livelihood from what 'goes before'; and conversely, these scenes which (like the lord) precede those that come after exist independently of what 'follows', even while in another sense they 'depend upon' what comes later.

As those images clearly suggest, the different parts of the play are mutually interdependent, and several further images hinting at this occur in Act III. When Achilles and Ulysses discuss reflection and self-reflection, for example, Achilles speaks of how a person's gaze needs to meet another's in order to behold itself, for 'eye to eye opposed/*Salutes each other with each other's form*' (III.iii. 107–8, my italics); only 'by reflection' in another's eyes can a man come to know himself, 'As when his virtues shining upon others/*Heat them, and they retort that heat again*/To the first giver' (III.iii. 100–2, my italics). This image of one thing heating another which 'retorts' the heat back to it is especially apposite to the way the play establishes its meanings, and so is Ulysses' elaboration of it when he speaks of how a man must 'communicate his parts to others' in order to know them by beholding them

      formed in th' applause
Where th' are extended; [which], like an arch, reverb'rate
The voice again; or, like a gate of steel

Fronting the sun, receives and renders back
His figure and his heat.

                                                    (III.iii. 119–23)

On this analogy, the later scenes of the play do not
effectively strike off or cancel or derealise the earlier love
scenes; rather, they 'reverb'rate/The voice again', 'receive
and render back' the 'heat' of those previous scenes. Or, to
put it in terms of a later conversation which re-echoes
Ulysses' phrase, the various scenes *take* significance from
each other and *give* to each other:

Cressida   In kissing, do you render or receive?
Patroclus Both take and give.

                                                    (IV.v. 36–7)

And once again the point applies equally to the way the
different parts within each scene or dialogue 'co-act', and to
the interaction of the different parts which make up the
whole play.

The immediate point in question here is quite what one
makes of the central love scenes, how they strike us as we
watch. One important feature of them all is that they are cast
teleologically, at least in the sense that they include an
always implicit recognition, carried in the dramatic
language, of the possibility and indeed the overwhelming
likelihood of this love ending in 'swooning destruction' or
fraying out to nought. This provides the basis of all
reductive reading of these scenes. But knocking against that
possibility is the contrary one, just as strongly voiced in the
lovers' speeches, that this love may flourish and 'keep [its]
constancy in plight and youth,/Outliving beauty's outward,
with a mind/That doth renew swifter than blood decays'. To
watch and listen to the drama here is to feel the constant
friction between these two possibilities, each intensified by
its quarrel with the other. Taken together in all their at-
oddsness, they make up the two main 'parts' in the 'good

broken music' of these scenes—music all the more unnerving because it does *not* resolve into a comfortably single sourness or sweetness, but is always liable suddenly to veer in or out of tune.

The contrast between the casual teasing persiflage of Act III Scene i and the deeper vibrancy of Act III Scene ii can be felt at once—and even though the comic edge is as sharp as ever. Troilus' opening speeches here are keyed and pitched differently from any in the play so far, his voice hushed, awed—'I am giddy'—amazed to discover in himself a fearful excitement beyond any he has known; and Cressida, whom we last saw in Act I Scene ii resolving not to show her love, is likewise (according to Pandarus' bulletin) flushed by a last-minute tumult of desire and trepidation:

> She's making her ready, she'll come straight; you must be witty now. She does so blush, and fetches her wind so short, as if she were fray'd with a sprite. I'll fetch her.
> (III.ii. 28–31)

In so describing Cressida, Pandarus equally reveals himself, and the emphatic tread of his chuckling prose is like a burlesque version of the lovers' high-strung breathless expectancy. The Cressida whose heart flutters wildly as she 'fetches her breath as short as a new-ta'en sparrow' strikes Pandarus' lascivious bird-catcher's eye as simply 'the prettiest villain', all the more delectable for her novice-nerved confusion. Troilus, far from being wittily detached and in command of the situation, finds himself overmastered by 'even such a passion' as hers, beyond his voluntary control, so that he feels like a vassal 'at unawares encount'ring/The eye of majesty' (even if her majesty is escorted by Pandarus); while she, on encountering his eye, is all the more unregally abashed and tremulous behind her veil. Cressida is to Troilus here the exact and perfect answer to the kind of love he feels, and he to hers. The actuality of their 'passion' is as much the focus of our attention as the actuality of Pandarus' very different outlook and experience, and indeed both the delicacy and vigour of the drama here comes from the tensions between all three.

It is a mistake therefore to suppose that Pandarus dominates the scene or brings the tone of it down to his level of ducks-in-the-river practicality. As with Thersites, so with Pandarus, there will doubtless always be some members of the audience for whom the most basic, illusion-free, lowest-common-denominator view will seem the truest. But nevertheless, it is clearly the case with Pandarus here that the lovers' presence and demeanour equally afford a perspective on *his*. Their youth and freshness wrinkles him the more by contrast, and partly because of this disparity between his age and theirs, his presence makes the scene not only funnier but more edgy, more jarring and more touching as well. Although he sees Cressida purely from his masculine 'bawd' point of view, for example, it is he who repeatedly draws attention to the blushes that express her innermost feelings ('She does so blush'; 'Come, come, what need you blush?'; 'What, blushing still!')—blushes which Pandarus clearly relishes (perhaps even partly invents, self-chafingly, to urge her on) and which he doubtless deepens a shade further by remarking their conspicuity. But to the lovers themselves (and to us watching them) Cressida's blushing betrays her desire, anxiety and embarrassment, all at once. It attests the conflux in her heart and veins of a timidity that makes her 'draw backward' and the boldness that propels her forward to the self-surrender of a love freely given and received. Rather than working simply to deflate, deride and de-romanticise the lovers' encounter, the comic ironies of the scene thus also work to bring out its deeper undercurrents: Pandarus' garrulousness, his urgent coaxings and noisy instructions serve to accentuate by contrast the sheer intensity of their emotions, beyond the limits of his jocular farmyard imagination, and far removed from the easy familiarities of Paris and 'my Nell' in the previous scene. Pandarus' bawdy patter both there and here thus underlines the disparity between the wordly drolleries of those two lovers (seven years on in their affair) and the nervous energy of this younger pair for whom this whole experience is new. Suddenly together for the first time, they are overwhelmed. Bereft of words, they gaze at each other in wondering silence, then passionately embrace and kiss—as all the while Pandarus keeps up his non-stop nudging commentary.

From such tensions as these, within and between all three of them, the liveliness of the drama here springs and keeps renewing itself through all its fluctuations and complications of tone and shifts of emphasis. It is hard to characterise these without slightly distorting them in one way or another. Here, however, some remarks of Hazlitt's in his luminous discussion of *Troilus* in his *Characters of Shakespear's Plays* (c. 1817) can help one see where the drama's strength and complexity lie:

> There is no *double entendre* in the characters of Chaucer: they are either quite serious or quite comic. In Shakespear the ludicrous and ironical are constantly blended with the stately and the impassioned.... Shakespear never committed himself to his characters.... He has no prejudices for or against them.... His genius was dramatic.... He saw both sides of a question, the different views taken of it according to the different interests of the parties concerned, and he was at once an actor and spectator in the scene.... He made infinite excursions to the right and the left.
> (*The Complete Works of William Hazlitt*, ed. P. P. Howe, vol. 4, London and Toronto 1930, p. 225)

This brings out well the way the whole of *Troilus* is a kind of double entendre, as registered in large matters like the characterisation and in small local details of language and scenic form. It is important therefore not to collapse its doubleness into singleness—for example, by pouncing on

all the ribaldries and double entendres with which the love
scenes are riddled and supposing it is enough to snigger at it
all, instead of also noticing what else there is to be
responded to at the same time. (The opposite problem, of
ignoring the ironies, is equally distorting.)

Thus, for instance, there is no shortage of derisory (ha ha
ha) readings, or moralistic (tisk tisk) ones, in which much is
made of Troilus as a type of 'sexual gourmet' whose 'febrile
lust' and mad idolatry in allowing his passion to triumph
over his reason are all there is to observe (from a distance)
and be titillated or scandalised by—as if, having seen in Act I
that he is rather an absurd, 'flawed' lover and that Cressida is
rather a calculating and 'defective' one, we need only sit
back in pang-free no-surprises comfort and watch this
simple diagnosis simply confirmed. Discussions and
productions showing Troilus as predominantly a ludicrous
figure and Cressida as an obvious vamp (e.g. 'sweltering with
concupiscence', as one reviewer described Dorothy Tutin's
performance in the RSC production in 1960) tend, in effect,
to reduce its double entendres to single ones. The reverse of
this has the same effect: for example, of sentimentalising and
simplifying by overemphasising the 'romantic' aspects and
screening out the subversive ironies.

The underswell of ribaldry throughout the love scenes is
continually capsizing and threatening to engulf the frail craft
of less strongly seasoned possiblities of experience, but this
does not mean that either invalidates the other. The play's
sense of sexual longings is neither prurient nor supercilious,
and just as it does not present the lovers simply from a
Pandarean perspective nor, for example, does it express a
Ulyssean disdain or abhorrence of all 'appetites' as
essentially reprehensible, destructive, evil, wolvish. It
realises that human appetite can indeed be ugly, nihilistic;
but it also—as here with Troilus and Cressida—conceives
their 'appetite' as something vital and healthy, of positive
value. Their love is shown as arising directly from their taste
for one another, from the quasi-electrical charge of sexual

attraction between them, which is prior to any considerations of 'truth', 'honour', 'faith'. The Cressida who can't help confessing that she was 'won', not by Troilus' honour or his valour, but 'with the first glance that ever— ...' (she breaks off, not saying if it happened on her first sight of him or his first glance at her or their first exchange of glances), is clearly a very different young woman from, say, the Desdemona for whom desiring, honouring and consecrating her life to Othello are indivisibly one and the same ('I saw Othello's visage in his mind;/And to his honours and his valiant parts/Did I my soul and fortunes consecrate': *Othello*, I.iii. 252–4). And on the other hand this impulsive Cressida, whose thoughts are 'like unbridled children, grown/Too headstrong for their mother' is also significantly unlike the Helen 'proud to be [Hector's] servant', whose inimitably languid 'yea's' and precious rhymes and royal plurals we heard in her closing speech to Paris in the previous scene:

> Yea, what he shall receive of us in duty
> Gives us more palm in beauty than we have,
> Yea, overshines ourself.
>
> (III.i. 149–51)

There is nothing primly censorious about the play's interest in 'what is', nor for example does it snidely smirk at this Troilus who so fervently wants to swear to things before they happen, to pledge an eternity of troth to his perfect Cressida, whose white enchanting fingers have driven him madly hot with desire.

Part of what makes this scene so fine is the way Shakespeare remains, in Hazlitt's phrase, 'at once an actor and spectator in the scene', for the dialogue sustains a complex double perspective and double entendre all through. Shakespeare's debunking spirit, so to speak, is constantly competing with his valuing spirit, and the great thing is that neither side wins. The drama's richness comes from their quarrel, which it also activates in us as we watch. Throughout these central scenes it is as if Shakespeare is writing both with and against the grain: he keeps framing the ironies so that they deflect or counter our impulses of imaginative sympathy, and yet the writing frequently achieves an accent of genuine pathos which challenges and undermines the easy detached knowingness to which the proleptic ironies appeal. It is not a question of the play being even-handed or taking a balanced view, for the thing is much less stable and static than that suggests—far more changeful and surprising, as again Hazlitt's (rather exaggerated but very suggestive) comparison of Shakespeare with his great English predecessor finely brings out:

> Chaucer's mind was consecutive, rather than discursive ... Shakespear saw every thing by intuition. Chaucer had a great variety of power, but he could do only one thing at once.... His ideas were kept separate, labelled, ticketed and parcelled out in a set form, in pews and compartments by themselves. *They did not play into one another's hands. They did not re-act upon one another, as the blower's breath moulds the yielding glass. There is something hard and dry in them. What is the most wonderful thing in Shakespear's faculties in their excessive sociablity, and how they gossiped and compared notes together.*
>
> (Hazlitt, p. 226; my italics)

This sociability of Shakespeare's faculties as they gossip and compare notes and make infinite excursions to the right and the left means that his audience's minds need to be fairly limber to keep up with all the swift 'transitions' and 'glancing lights', as Hazlitt puts it. Interestingly, Hazlitt wonders in passing whether these may be excessive: 'if any thing [Shakespeare] is too various and flexible: to full of ... salient points ... perhaps ... too volatile and heedless.' Certainly, the play is very demanding. Often, it requires that we do a sort of double or treble take. At any rate, to see it as single-mindedly 'anti-romantic', as opposed to Chaucer's 'romantic' poem, is for these reasons (as I see it) to oversimplify—just as it oversimplifies the play and its relationship to its Homeric 'source' to describe it categorically as 'anti-heroic'. Such hard and fast distinctions tend to blur as much as they clarify—and this is especially unfortunate when what gets blurred is the marvellously 'mix'd of all stuffs' drama of these central scenes.

The prose dialogue between the lovers, following Pandarus' exit in Act III Scene ii (line 55), for example, marks another change of pitch and tempo as they speak of long-felt wishes and fears—wishes feared to be unattainable, and fears they wish and pray to dispel. The pressure of other moments—what's past and what's to come—bears heavily on both of them in this momentous here and now:

> *Troilus*   O Cressid, how often have I wish'd me thus!
> *Cressida* Wish'd my lord! The gods grant—O my lord!
>   (III.ii. 58–9)

But it is he, whose aches of unfulfilled longing arose from her fear-prompted holding-off, who now seeks gently to allay her fears, to persuade her to trust his truth. Compared with his rapid-pulsed, short-breathed verse at the scene's beginning, the tone and rhythms of his speeches now express a new fluency and self-possession, which not even her grim melancholy foreboding can shake:

> *Troilus*   What should they grant? What makes this
>   pretty abruption? What too curious dreg
>   espies my sweet lady in the fountain of our
>   love?
> *Cressida* More dregs than water, if my fears have eyes.
>   (III.ii. 62–4)

The apprehensive youth who before their first kiss had expressed his own quite different anxieties ('Death, I fear me

...', 'I fear it much; and I do fear besides ...') now speaks
soothingly—'O, let my lady apprehend no fear!'—and
authoritatively: 'In all Cupid's pageant there is presented no
monster'. The green-eyed one and sundry others likewise
unappeasable seem to have 'slipp'd out of [his]
contemplation' (II.iii.24). Cressida's responses hereabouts
sound several rather jarring notes, trivialising his anxiety
and trying to appear very experienced but not managing to
conceal her own uncertainty and brittleness. Though full of
doubt, she is keen to be set at ease: 'Nor nothing monstrous
neither?':

> Troilus   Nothing, but our undertakings when we vow
> to weep seas, live in fire, eat rocks, tame tigers;
> thinking it harder for our mistress to devise
> imposition enough than for us to undergo any
> difficulty imposed. *This is the monstruosity in
> love, lady, that the will is infinite, and the
> execution confin'd; that the desire is boundless, and
> the act a slave to limit.*
>
> (III.ii. 74–80, my italics)

The epigrammatic force of this makes it very arresting,
and on reflection this account of 'the monstruosity in love'
can be seen to point to a central preoccupation of the whole
play, though here again one needs to beware of de-
dramatising the drama, as it were, or foisting upon it certain
certainties which it more tough-mindedly interrogates and
thus prompts us to ponder, question, apprehend in a new
way. The play puts so much stress upon 'limit' and upon the
'confines' of execution that it has often been taken as
comprehensively demonstrating these bitter facts—as if it
endorsed without qualification Agamemnon's remark in
Act I Scene iii that 'The ample proposition that hope
makes/In all designs begun on earth below/Fails in the
promis'd largeness.' On this reading, the play is seen as
insisting that the 'failure' is more real and more significant

than any 'hope' or 'aim'; the stark contrast between boundless desire and the limited bounds of action is seen as cuttingly ironic, its effect being to undermine 'desire', 'design', 'intent', 'wish', 'hope'—as if the very sequence of 'will' running up against 'limit' speaks its own valuation of the two, desire proving helpless and even absurd in the face of everything that restricts or blocks it. Thus the play as a whole is seen as expressing an acute, sardonic and even cynical irony at the inevitable failure of human aims, and the futility of all aspirations. (Some critics take this a stage or two further, arguing that Agamemnon's remark may imply a metadramatic critique of the play and indeed of play-making in general.)

But here again, the evidence of the early scenes and especially of Acts III and IV suggests that such a view of the play is overstated. For *Troilus* is much less dispirited, less inert, and less merely illustrative than that—and it is worthwhile trying to get clear why such an account sells it short.

(iii)

Even within Act III Scene ii itself Troilus' way of describing 'the monstruosity in love' suggests that the play's sense of this is dynamic. For one thing, he gives equal weight to each fact of experience: *'the desire is boundless, and the act a slave to limit'* (my italics). '*And*', not '*but*'. His point is that 'the monstruosity' involves the co-existence of both. His formulation does not concede that the reality of 'limit' effectively cancels the reality of desire, nor that limit annuls the value of desire. In each of his parallel phrases his pivotal 'and' poises the two terms, makes them meet their match, as it were, so that they confront and answer each other, exist in tension against each other. Neither is granted supremacy over its opposite.

What this suggests more broadly—and this scene as a

whole amply bears it out—is that the play itself is equally interested in what lies on either side of Troilus' 'and'—'on one and other side', to use the Prologue's phrase. Moreover, as with Troilus and Cressida themselves, or the Greeks and the Trojans, its concern is not just with each separately but 'on both sides' in their interrelationship: its imagining of each is inextricable from its imagining of the other. Throughout the play, everyone's desire is sharpened on the whetstone of limit as each of them imagines, like Paris, what he would do 'were I alone to pass the difficulties,/And had as ample power as I have will'. (Thersites, smarting from Ajax's blows, fantasises an ideal world in which 'I could beat him, whilst he rail'd at me!') For of course their boundless desires express the wish to transcend the bounds of time and circumstance, to outfly the limits of execution, which (in Ulysses' terms) 'like a bourn, a pale, a shore', confines their 'spacious and dilated' dreams. Having only finite powers they long to 'fly' on 'painted wings'; 'that spirit of his/In aspiration lifts him from the earth'. The play's apprehension of all this, the sheer vitality and power of its language of *desire* needs to be taken into account, for it is in this sense quite Marlovian—and of course here and there Shakespeare pays tribute to Marlowe and seems to have him specifically in mind. '*Would it were otherwise*', mutters Thersites: 'Sfoot, I'll learn to conjure and raise devils, but I'll see some issue of my ... execrations'. Not despite but because of what Troilus calls the 'difficulty imposed', they all dream of surmounting it; and the play is as full of yearning, wishing, 'If ...', 'would I could ...', as it is of shackling 'musts' and 'cannot's—full of subjunctives, conditionals, hypotheses, which push *against* the facts of confinement even in acknowledging them. The dramatic language is everywhere imbued with the energies of desire, and nowhere more so than in these central scenes. Nor are such energies valued the less because of their continual and inevitable collisions with 'limits'.

This suggests a further point which needs taking into

account—that the play's apprehension of 'the monstruosity' is not fixed or static, not the same all through. It
changes and deepens from one scene to the next, one Act to
the next; and that progressive deepening coincides with—is
one aspect of—the unfolding logic of the dramatic action
whereby, in dramatising the alterations in the characters'
experience, the play ever more acutely realises the nexus
between desires and limits, and excites in us a
correspondingly acute realisation of this too. This is the
focus of most of its comic as of its tragic awareness; and the
fact that these are often coterminous is one reason why the
play is so demanding—and so rewarding—to watch, and
also why its conception of 'the monstruosity' becomes by
the end much more profoundly unsettling than Marlowe's,
for instance, or Ben Jonson's or Middleton's.

Certainly, Shakespeare's thinking in *Troilus* about the
relationship between desires and limits is as various as there
are moods and moments of experience in the play. Troilus'
wish to reassure Cressida here, for example, leads him to
speak in a tone of equanimity quite unlike his exquisite
super-sensitive jitters only moments before, and still more
unlike his racked extravagant protests in the opening scene,
when he blenched at 'suff'rance' and chafed against the
confined execution of his infinite will, only to change his
tune again by equably joining 'the sport abroad' instead of
staying at home as he'd choose 'if "would I might" were
"may"' (I.i. 112). Here, miraculously, in Act III Scene ii, his
'would I might' *is* 'may', as Cressida's consent 'gives wings
to [his] propension' (cf. II.ii. 132–3); and thus, although he is
soon dreaming of still higher perfections ('O that I thought it
could be …'), there is for him at this moment 'nothing
monstrous' about 'the monstruosity' in love; and yet a few
scenes later, and still more by the end, he will find it a
hideous 'monster' indeed. Each of these diverse ways of
experiencing desire and limit is dramatised in relation to all
the others, including Thersites' characteristic rage,
Agamemnon's bland acceptance, Cressida's dread, and so

on. And our own experience is witnessing, weighing and responding to each in turn is correspondingly diverse, growing knottier and more troubled as the play proceeds.

Much of the interest of Act III, Scene ii centres in its lively apprehension of the lovers apprehensiveness about what they are embarking on—especially Cressida's, as she ventures into the wild and wandering flood. All the tonal modulations here trace the ebb and flow of her confidence, her alternating faith and doubt in the future of their love; and the scene mounts beautifully to its climax at the end via her hesitations, her waxings and wanings of trust in Troilus and in herself. Her fantasy of 'more dregs than water' is soon flushed out by his fresh assurances of love's capacity, and the cheekier, bawdier worldly-wisdom bubbling up in her replies spills into laughter which brings new 'boldness' to declare the secrets of her heart. But even here she 'draws backward', alarmed at her self-exposure: she startles Pandarus and dismays Troilus by threatening to leave, despite her lover's attempts to hold her by stopping her mouth with kisses—'albeit', as he says, 'sweet music issues thence'. Typically, their discomforts here are both funny and moving. And thus the scene's sweetest music is held off till its close, when this battle of fear and desire within her is temporarily resolved, and at last there can be a moment of harmony, in their playfully earnest fancy of 'warring' in a contest of right against right—Troilus declaring himself an eternal touchstone of faithfulness, and she affirming her 'match and weight' of constancy in love by proclaiming herself, 'If I be false', a timeless exemplar of falsehood. They are well tuned now. Each voice perfectly echoes the happiness in the other's. And to complicate the harmonics there is also a part for Pandarus to sing as he rowdily takes their hands and they whisper their amens, in an impromptu little ceremony of a marriage of true minds, to 'crown up and sanctify' their love's everlastingness.

'Prophet may you be!': listening to the three of them here we cannot but flinch at recognising the fateful accuracy of

their words about Troilus' truth, Cressida's falsity and
Pandarus' going-between; and because of this it has often
been claimed that they themselves likewise foresee—
consciously predict—what is to come. It is said that they
'step out of character' here, stand 'outside' their story, view
it from the same perspective of hindsight as we do in
witnessing it. But such a reading projects onto them an
awareness that they do not have, and in so doing it mis-hears
the extraordinary 'good broken music' of this moment,
wherein the very words in which Cressida tunefully affirms
her truth express the horribly out-of-tune possibility of its
collapse. The sense here of a monstrous incongruity
between 'desire' and 'limit', 'will' and 'execution' is ours,
not theirs. The subjunctive casting of her speech ('Prophet
may you be!'; 'If I be false ... let them say'), echoed by
Pandarus' subjunctives ('If ever you prove false ... let ... let
... let ... let ...') is not at all equivalent to 'when I am' or
'when you are'; and to mistake the grammatical mood is to
mistake the mood in the other sense—to falsify the
characters' mood and thus to falsify the play's. *Not* knowing
the future that will become their famous history, they
joyfully defy the taciturnity of nature's secrets, seeking to
certify the permanence of their love by declaring their desire
for it to be limitless. But their 'ignoring'—their unknowing
and their ardent repudiation of contrary possibilities—is
what makes the scene so heart-rending to watch. Cressida,
speaking of a future in which present realities, like the
stones of Troy, will be worn away, grated to dusty nothing
in a world of forgetfulness and self-forgetting, trusts
implicitly that her faith will prove immune to all the
erosions that her words so poignantly evoke. Like Troilus
here, she trusts the fountain, forgets the spectre of the dregs.
The vulnerability of their love now matches the amplitude
of their hopes for it, and the drama impels us to grasp (as
they cannot) both facts at once.

(iv)

By highlighting the gaps as well as the overlaps between the various characters' experience here and our own in witnessing theirs, the scene evokes a feeling of pity inseparably mixed with relief and pleasure at the lovers' delight, which is complicated but not reduced by Pandarus' raunchy gloating gusto as he packs them off to bed. As with Cassandra's premonition and all the other prefigurative speeches in the play—'I spy', 'You spy! What do you spy?' (III.i. 87–8)—their own words in sealing their love make us spy in its fountain those chances of disaster which they (like the Princes in the debate) resolve to disbelieve, and our minds—like Achilles' in the next scene—are 'troubled, like a fountain stirr'd'. But here as on all the other occasions where the dregs and shadows of the past and future cloud the jubilance of the extant moment, the dramatic irony expresses and excites, not a Thersites-like sneering mirth, but a sharpened sense of the pity in it—the piteousness of their fears, their hopes and their blissful ignorance.

The run of scenes that follows set an even sharper edge on this and throws up unignorably the central question of whether our sense of the reality and value of this love is changed by the knowledge of its frailty, by the fact that it will not last. As with many of the previous scenes, including Act III Scene ii, so with these (III.iii, IV.i, IV.ii), the internal organisation of each accentuates the tensions between the various characters and between their consciousness and ours as we watch; and again these are compounded by the way each scene is 'set by other', each one 'knocking' against those on either side.

Some of this abrasiveness is lost, however, if the run of scenes is broken at the end of Act III Scene ii to allow for an interval. This is often done in modern productions of the play, and there are good reasons for it, as proponents have pointed out. As Emrys Jones puts it, Pandarus' final couplet addressed to the audience 'fittingly rounds off the [play's

first] movement with an air of finality' and rudely breaks the
dramatic illusion ('And Cupid grant all tongue-tied maidens
here,/Bed, chamber, pander, to provide this gear!'), effects
which make for a satisfying symmetry when, in a kind of
'structural rhyming', the 'second part' likewise closes with
Pandarus addressing the audience in lewdly winking
couplets, at the play's end (Emrys Jones, *Scenic Form in
Shakespeare*, Oxford 1971, pp. 82–3). Certainly, our powers
of concentration need some rest and recreation somewhere
along the way; and because the lovers' coming-together
clearly climaxes the play's first half, the scene-break here,
which switches attention to the Greek camp—new matter,
in a new key—seems a natural place to take a pause.

But without disputing the play's articulation of a two-part
structure (both formal and imaginative), which makes itself
felt whether or not the performance pauses at this point, it is
arguable that an interval here inappropriately softens the
sense of disruption and rude interruption caused by the
immediate contiguity of these two scenes. Whereas Cupid
and Pandarus kindly 'grant' and 'provide' such reliefs as the
lovers desire, the play seems less amenable towards its
audience. By design, it 'justles roughly by/All time of
pause'. As the lovers go off to bed together we naturally wish
for an easeful interval or a scene free of any stressful bearing
on their love. Instead, we are confronted with a business-
matter which seals its doom.

Swiftly and casually, the pleasures and hopes of the
previous scene are overthrown. There is no preamble and
no warning. The old man who steps forward is bent on
having *his* desire fulfilled without delay ('*Now*, Princes ...');
he recites aloud from bitter memory the moral accounts he
has kept to prove the Greeks' indebtedness to him,
itemising every cost he has incurred on their behalf—'I have
abandon'd Troy, left my possession,/Incurr'd a traitor's
name ...'—and for such faith-breaking 'service' he claims
remuneration 'now' from those whose compensation pay-
outs have thus far failed in the promised largeness. His voice

sounds tight with resentful mistrust. Agamemnon in reply does not deign to dignify the complainant with a name, but his sneering stress on 'Troyan'—'What wouldst thou of us, Troyan?'—bespeaks his scorn for the man he seems to regard as a sort of broker-lackey, a traitorous alien who will never be one of 'us'.

It is assumed that we know from Chaucer that this is Calchas; but any residually hopeful doubt is promptly struck off by the proposal that the Greeks exchange the war prisoner Antenor for 'my Cressid', in a trade-off as expeditious as its grammar: Antenor 'shall buy my daughter; and her presence/Shall quite strike off all service I have done'. (His phrases jarringly echo those repeatedly used in relation to Helen—the idea of 'buying' and of debts or damages being 'struck off', 'cut off', 'wiped off'.) The Greeks do not pause to discuss the proposal. (Nor—despite Calchas' point that Troy has always 'denied' the exchange 'oft desired' by the Greeks—is it part of Shakespeare's purpose to include any Trojan debate, as in Chaucer, over whether to keep Cressida or yield her up, though Dryden took it upon himself to introduce such a debate between Hector and Troilus.) In Agamemnon's curt assent—'Let Diomedes bear [Antenor],/And bring us Cressid hither'— the play starkly accentuates the shocking speed of the settlement and its gratuitous injuriousness. Only moments before, the boisterous broker Pandarus had been crowing, 'Go to, a bargain made; seal it, seal it', but the last thing on any of their minds as the lovers pledged their faith was the chance of their hopes being crushed by anyone else's bargains, least of all one involving the enemy. Within seconds of its first being mentioned, the 'interchange' is under way; and the Greeks turn their attention to the (for them) more urgent problem of how to make Achilles' 'will' bendy and supple to serve their own.

Shakespeare might well have chosen to present and arrange this material very differently—for instance, by delaying Calchas' demand until after the business with

Achilles, or by having it reported in Troy (rather than dramatising it directly) and perhaps even synchronising the lovers' reception of the news with the audience's. But his conception is far more subtle-potent than any such alternatives. This abrupt unbuffered juxtaposing of the lovers' 'rapture' and the exchange deal that will shatter it gives maximum force to the collision between their desires and Calchas', while neither party has any knowledge of the other's contrary will. Calchas, apparently unaware of the state of his daughter's heart, desires only the comfort of her presence to alleviate the griefs of his own, but in his saying that this will 'strike off' his service to the Greeks 'in most accepted pain', the play makes us seeringly aware of the most *un*accepted pain this deal must cause Troilus and Cressida—a pain of which no one in this scene has the faintest inkling. Indeed, this is a key dramatic function of the scene-change: it produces in *our* minds an acute sense of conflict which is given no expression within the play until the lovers' later realisation that they must part, 'and suddenly'.*

The realisation thrust upon us that the lovers' joy is fated to become a casualty of the war does not diminish our sense of its beauty and worth; indeed, their brief happiness now seems the more precious in view of its imminent loss. By

---

*For anyone producing the play it may be worth the cost of losing some of the nicer symmetries and foregoing any break here, in order to stress this dire pivotal effect of the scene-change; but this leaves the question of where to give actors and audience a necessary rest. To create as strong as possible an impression of the play as a single integral whole (i.e. to bring out strongly both its forward drive and the sense of 'abruption' and disjunction so vital to it) it may work best to have two brief breaks at points that are not structurally critical, so as to allow maximum concentration on the scenic runs and turns that matter most. One place for a refreshing but minimally interferent pause is after the Trojan council (II.ii) which ends climactically and prospectively, resuming in Act II Scene iii with a salutary 'performance' of Thersites' 'heaving spleen' (the ironies would be slightly blunted by this, but not too much). And the end of Act IV Scene iv (Troilus' and Cressida's parting) affords another not-too-distracting pause, for again this moment is climactic and the scene closes prospectively with the Trojans 'mak[ing] ready straight' to 'tend to Hector's heels' in the chivalric contest of Act IV Scene v (which scene also strikingly inaugurates a new epoch for Cressida, amongst the Greeks).

burdening the audience with such knowledge while the
lovers offstage remain innocent of it, the play thus sets them
at a distance even while it generates a strong current of
sympathy for them, which reaches a new pitch when they
next appear in the dawn after their night of loving (IV.ii),
still—in Chaucer's phrase—'ful unavysed of [their] woo
comynge'. Like Act III Scene ii, this dawn scene is jarringly
played off against the preceding ones which comprise its
immediate context—the remainder of the scene in the
Greek camp (III.iii) and another in Troy—both of which
stress the harsh inclemencies of the war-world wherein their
love (like all the love in the play) exists and must find its limit
and its destiny. Ulysses' manipulative cynicism not only
chafes Achilles with the knowledge that his 'fame is
shrewdly gor'd', but leaves an overriding impression of the
Greek camp to which Cressida must go as a place where no
privacy escapes the eyes of espionage and where nothing is
safe from the trampling hoofs of envious emulation and
mockery—an impression given its final twist by Thersites'
raucous 'pageant of Ajax'. 'Why, but he is not in this tune, is
he?' Achilles asks, as they all double up with laughter:

> *Thersites*   No, but he's out o' tune thus. What music will
> be in him when Hector has knock'd his brains
> out, I know not; but I am sure, none; unless the
> fiddler Apollo get his sinews to make catlings
> on.
>
> (III.iii. 296–9)

But some of the most disaffectedly out of tune music
comes in Act IV Scene i with Diomedes' arrival in Troy on
his mission to exchange 'the enfreed Antenor' for 'the fair
Cressid', when he answers Paris' naïvely courteous query as
to 'who ... deserves fair Helen best,/Myself or Menelaus?',
by denouncing Paris as a 'lecher', Menelaus a 'puling
cuckold', and Helen 'a whore'.

Diomedes' diatribe is extreme and unmitigated; and

because of its intensity it has sometimes been taken as expressing the play's own ultimate judgement of all three, as if Shakespeare regards them as an abomination, and recoils from them, Helen especially, with the same primitive disgust as Diomedes' or Thersites'. Certainly, Diomedes' moral revulsion, expressed in grossly physical terms, has far greater poetic and dramatic force here than Paris' blandly evasive retort about buying and selling, and Diomedes' sense of the appalling *cost* of the war is repeatedly confirmed elsewhere. But like every other valuation in the play his judgement expresses something of the valuer as well as of the thing valued: Diomedes is the man who sees Helen and the others in these terms and in this tone of absolute contempt. And like every other valuation in the play it is itself dramatically weighed and valued in relation to other and often quite contrary ways of perceiving and evaluating Helen's reality or that of Cressida or of love or the war, and so on, which are as much part of the whole drama as Diomedes' own at this point. (The vilifier of Paris' 'lechery' is soon bent on enjoying a little lechery himself.) His bitter denunciation sorts oddly with his affable 'And that's my mind too' when Aeneas brightly referred to Paris' 'bed-mate' at the start of the scene; and it sorts even more oddly with his prompt alacrity in Act III Scene iii in accepting his war commission from Agamemnon: 'This shall I undertake; and 'tis a burden/Which I am proud to bear'. That expression is strangely reminiscent of Helen's own, "t will make us proud to be his servant, Paris' (III.i. 148); and indeed the memory of that scene with her comes vividly to mind again as Diomedes reviles her here in Paris' presence, her beauty and the touch of her white enchanting fingers now savagely denigrated as 'her contaminated carrion weight'.

This image of Helen as a putrefying carcase is horribly out of tune with the frivolous music of that earlier scene; it is (in Troilus' phrase) 'tun'd too sharp' in bitterness; but its potency is no greater than that of the dramatic language of other quite differently tuned speeches in previous scenes—Troilus', for instance ('I am giddy ...'), or Thersites' or Hector's or Ulysses' or Pandarus'—none of which simply cancels or invalidates the others. To Diomedes, Helen is simply a 'whore', personally responsible for all the lives 'spent' and 'sunk' in her defence; he neglects to inquire far into her defenders' responsibility—Greeks' and Trojans' alike—for setting so high a value on a worthless harlot and wasting so many precious lives in such a cause. But the play does not neglect to inspect these things. Its thinking about the whole matter, which includes and weighs Diomedes' judgement here and such contrary ones as those expressed in the council scenes, probes deeper into the underground roots of categorical judgements like these, seeking to the bottom of what impels such men as these particular Trojans and Greeks (including Diomedes) to engage in such a war, and to hazard their lives on the chance of winning, at whatever 'costly loss'.

(v)

The scenes in which the lovers' joy is rudely interrupted (IV.ii–iv) are obviously crucial ones, and not just in terms of the progress of the plot. They mark a new development in the dramatic action. What happens to Troilus and Cressida here—and more especially what happens *in* them—changes the nature of their experience of love; and in dramatising this play itself suddenly becomes more intense as well, a change palpably realised in the greater concentration of the verse, particularly in Act IV Scene iv on the verge of the lovers' parting. As with all the others, of course, these love scenes can be played in a variety of ways, being ambiguous enough to warrant quite a range of different emphases. But it is important not to trivialise the emotional charge of the poetry here, which contributes directly to the play's power as a whole.

Throughout these scenes the sudden fluctuations of tone and pitch are very striking, and each thus sharply 'set by other, more for other semeth': the shift from Diomede's antagonistic virulence in Act IV Scene i to the lovers' mutual tenderness in Act IV Scene ii, for instance, and the similarly disconcerting shifts *within* each of the following scenes. Again, the very abruptness of these is part of their dramatic point. In Act IV Scene ii, for example, the bold simple scene-design throws maximum stress on the swift reversal between the opening and the close, as the lovers' joy devolves into shock and wretchedness, a joy 'no sooner got but lost', transmuted to dismay. And this sudden switch of mood from 'wele' to 'woe' goes with an equally striking intensification, from the soft-voiced, rather low-key exchanges with which the scene begins, to the violent tumult of distress—Cressida's—in which it culminates. The extremity of her grief, and of Troilus' in Act IV Scene iv, is poignantly accentuated by being thus dramatically set against their quieter joy and laughing playfulness only moments before.

Thus the scene begins without any great high-soaring declarations of fulfilled love—nothing to match Desdemona's or Othello's passionate intensity, for example (as in *Othello*, I.iii or II.i), or Antony's magnificence ('Here is my space./Kingdoms are clay ...', in *Antony and Cleopatra* I.i. 33–4). Compared with those, Troilus and Cressida's speeches here are far less exultant, more subdued—which not only suggests something about these particular lovers but also about this play which bears their names. Nor—and again it tells something of these lovers and this play—does the quality of the poetry they speak match the beautiful radiant simplicity of Perdita and Florizel's, for instance (as in *The Winter's Tale*, IV.iv): it is much more alloyed, mixed, impure, and, to our ears at least—though not to theirs—many of their phrases in their 'aubade' are ominously out of tune: 'cold', 'kill', 'venemous', 'tediously', 'catch cold', 'curse', 'pestilence', 'mocking', and so on. It is utterly

characteristic of the play that the voice of the 'lark' is here
companioned by that of 'the ribald crows': not just one kind
of music but two kinds, sounding simultaneously. To hear
only one—only lark or crow—is to mis-hear the scene.
(Cressida's part in particular is full of crowy notes.) It is also
characteristic of the play that the lovers' delight in being
together—which is so clearly manifest here in their voices,
faces, laughter, gestures—is expressed in terms of their
sense of its brevity, and that their wish to prolong it is
heightened by the consciousness that 'the morn is cold' and
they must part:

Cressida	Are you weary of me?
Troilus	O Cressida! but that the busy day,
	Wak'd by the lark, hath rous'd the ribald crows,
	And dreaming night will hide our joys no longer,
	I would not from thee.

(IV.i. 7–11)

Her question is as typical of her as his reply is of him; and
his yearning tone and syntax ('but that ... no longer,/I would
not ...') touchingly express the tension between their desire
to be together and the necessity of parting, which is the
play's main focus here, and which becomes more extreme in
both of them as the rest of this scene and its sequel now
unfolds. Aeneas had said in the previous scene,

Had I so good occasion to lie long
As you, Prince Paris, nothing but heavenly business
Should rob my bed-mate of my company.

(IV.i. 4–6)

But the unimpeded entry of the ribald crowing Pandarus—
'What's all the doors open here?'—is only the first
unheavenly business of 'the busy day/Wak'd by the lark',

which will rob them of each other's company, and only a thin partition of time and matter now protects them from it:

> [*One Knocks*]
> Cressida Who's that at door? ...
> [*Knock*]
> How earnestly they knock! ...
> Pandarus Who's there? What's the matter? Will you beat down the door?
>
> (IV.i. 35 et seq.)

Nowhere else does the play arouse a more painful sense of the wickerwork fragility of their love—its capacity to be broken into and broken up by 'the chance of war'; and nowhere more than in these scenes is its value more inseparably bound up in its frailty. Their grief is their realisation of everything that threatens it and their realisation that its worth—to them—is absolute.

This is one reason why it is important not to miss the way the formal structuring of the drama here brings out the force of Cressida's reaction as well as Troilus', giving it great prominence at the end of this scene, and again at the start of Act IV Scene iv. Even in hearing that she must go, the lovers are isolated from each other. Cressida remains off-stage when Troilus hears it from Aeneas, who delays the blow till the last moment—'we must give up... /The Lady Cressida'—while stressing that there can be no evasion: 'I scarce have leisure to salute you,/My matter is so rash'; 'There is at hand ... / ... Antenor/ ... and for him forthwith,/Ere the first sacrifice, within this hour,/We must ...'; 'They are at hand and ready to effect it'. Once again the play significantly distinguishes Troilus' way of experiencing the shock from Pandarus' and in turn from Cressida's own. Troilus' dazed, desolate, terse bitterness—'How my achievements mock me!'—is tellingly set against Pandarus' self-unconscious volubility: *his* consternation explodes outwards, finding self-comfort in angry blame of Antenor, the world and, above all, Cressida: 'Would thou hadst ne'er been born! I knew thou wouldst be his death! O, poor gentleman!'. Completely engrossed in his own distress—the reflex of Troilus'—Pandarus ignores her appeals to be told what is wrong, his denials fanning the desperation of her desire to know; and part of the dramatic effect of his reaction, which treats her feelings as of no account while sympathising entirely with Troilus'—'Twill be his death; ... he cannot bear it'—is precisely to bring out the unignorable actuality of her pain, the fact that *she* 'cannot bear it' any more than Troilus can.

For it is her storm of grief and defiance which dominates the scene's close, and in its raw violence there is no mistaking the love of Troilus which is its cause. This is why it is so significant and so memorable. Whatever else Cressida has been or may become, *this* is part of what she is. To regard her here as a whore-apparent or 'daughter of the game', and respond simply with a wry or knowing 'ha ha ha', is to ignore or invert the testimony of our eyes and ears. For this is Cressida—the young woman whom we saw in Acts I and III, yet changed by what has happened since then—the same, and not the same. Nothing in her 'draws backward' from Troilus now; her whole will is to 'reside' with him, and she has at this moment no 'unkind self, that it self will leave/To be another's fool' (III.ii. 145–6):

> I have forgot my father;
> I know no touch of consanguinity,
> No kin, no love, no blood, no soul so near me
> As the sweet Troilus.
>
> (IV.ii. 95–8)

Throughout her speech, the passionate *resistant* energy of her negatives positively declares the singleness of her will to stay in Troy and stay as she is—a desire never more boundless than in this crisis of realising all that contravenes it and would mark its limit. Thus the drama here centres in the headlong collision between what Pandarus sorrily insists upon—'Thou must be gone ... thou must be gone ... thou must to thy father, and be gone from Troilus ... Thou must'—and her outright refusal: 'I will not go ... I will not, uncle ... I will not go from Troy'. No longer now is 'the monstruosity in love' 'nothing monstrous': her 'infinite will' is not merely inseparable from, but experienced wholly in terms of all that would confine its execution. Against the spectre of her falsity 'if ever she leave Troilus' she insists that her love is indestructible; but the sobs with which she cleaves to him acknowledge her ultimate impotence in the face of that imperative, 'must', which has the power to break her. The inward-turning, self-disfiguring violence of her grief—poignantly reminiscent of Chaucer's Criseyde and Henryson's Cresseid—at once concedes and protests against the transmutation of all her self-trust into self-despair:

> I'll go in and weep—
> Tear my bright hair, and scratch my praised cheeks,
> Crack my clear voice with sobs and break my heart,
> With sounding 'Troilus'.
>
> (IV.ii. 104–8)

(vi)

It is a critical commonplace that *Troilus and Cressida*, like *Henry IV*, for example, *Hamlet* or the Sonnets, is incessantly concerned with time; but it is clear throughout these central scenes that this concern is not about abstractions like capital-letter Time and Mutability (as in Ulysses' famous generalisations in III.iii)—though this is how it is often discussed. The play's general thinking is everywhere rooted in particulars: in the various characters' particular experience of what it means to live in this world subject to

time and change, and above all here, the lovers' experience
of having their joy snatched away. The passage of time that is
suddenly bringing such extreme, unexpected changes has
already within a day's brief span wrought great changes in
both of them, and the fervour with which they identify
themselves with their new experience is significant.
Cressida, in the speech just quoted—'I have forgot my
father'—declares her love for Troilus to be incomparably
more important than any other tie; indeed, she claims to
'know' no other. The very completeness of 'I have *forgot*' is
revealing—and ominous. (The contrast with Cordelia, for
example, or Desdemona, is striking.) Her present feelings
not only dominate but replace all her previous ones, as she
cries out against the decree, 'I will not go'. Cressida's
resistant will is made more absolute by her recognition (and
the play's) of all that wars against it and is bound to defeat
it—as Paris pityingly insists to Troilus in Act IV Scene iii:
'The hour prefix'd/For her delivery ... /Comes fast upon';
although Paris wishes he 'could help', 'there is no help;/The
bitter disposition of the time/Will have it so' (IV.i. 49–51).
The same is true with Troilus too, as he realises and
passionately protests against their helplessness to escape
this 'injury of chance' or to prevent this daylight robbery of
everything they value. In stark contrast to such other about-
to-be-parted lovers as those in Donne's 'A Valediction:
Forbidding Mourning' or 'Sweetest love ...', their every
utterance is marked by a desperate sense of hurry and strain.

Troilus' reply to her question, 'And is it true that I must
go from Troy?' (IV.iv. 29ff), is the crucial speech in this
scene and a key one in the play as a whole, for in expressing
his experience of being forcibly jostled, robbed, scanted, it
also expresses what may be called the quintessential *Troilus
and Cressida* experience—that sense of violently clashing
energies, of violent 'desire ... still denied', which more and
more dominates our own experience of the dramatic action
from here on to the end. It is as if the play's sense of such
jostling momentarily converges with Troilus' own. Never

till now has the verse irresistibly drawn us like this into such
an experience of the 'monstruosity' in which its two aspects
are grasped simultaneously in and through each other: not
simply as desire *and* limit nor even as desire *becoming* 'a slave
to limit', but desire experienced in terms of limit and limit in
terms of desire. The two things are inseparable, each is a
form of the other, each is realised in its indomitable push
and enmity against the other:

Cressida	And is it true ... Is't possible?
Troilus	And suddenly; where injury of chance
	Puts back leave-taking, justles roughly by
	All time of pause, rudely beguiles our lips
	Of all rejoindure, forcibly prevents
	Our lock'd embrasures, strangles our dear
	vows
	Even in the birth of our own labouring breath.
	We two, that with so many thousand sighs
	Did buy each other, must poorly sell ourselves
	With the rude brevity and discharge of one.
	Injurious time now with a robber's haste
	Crams his rich thievery up, he knows not how.
	As many farewells as be stars in heaven,
	With distinct breath and consign'd kisses to
	them,
	He fumbles up into a loose adieu,
	And scants us with a single famish'd kiss,
	Distasted with the salt of broken tears.
Aeneas	[*Within*] My lord, is the lady ready?

(IV.iii. 28–47)

Passionate protest against what is happening is one and the
same as passionate longing; and what is longed for is
specified, imaginatively realised as a possibility, in the same
words which express the counter-reality of all that destroys
its chance to exist. It is a longing for a different way of *being*,
of being not justled, not prevented, not scanted, not put

back—a hunger indeed for a 'time of pause', for the chance of a proper leave-taking in which 'our lips', 'our embrasures', 'our vows', 'our breath' might express what they urgently need to say. Even as the violence of time and chance is felt as a kind of physical thuggery in those formidable active present-tense verbs—'justles', 'strangles', 'crams', 'fumbles up'—the oppositional energy of resistance is voiced with answering force against the injuries inflicted thus 'roughly', 'forcibly', 'rudely' (bluntly and disregardingly). For although 'chance' 'rudely beguiles our lips/Of all rejoindure'—cheats our lips, beguiles them of all chance to rejoin in more kisses and of all chance to remonstrate against this prevention—Troilus' speech is itself an impassioned rejoinder, forcibly objecting to every privation and negation: if not thus rudely prevented, 'our embrasures' would be 'lock'd'; if not thus bagged by a fumbling thief who loses distinction in his haste, every farewell kiss would be 'distinct' and treasured to the utmost.

The intensity of yearning here, which is so characteristic of Troilus, at once links and contrasts this moment with previous ones such as 'I am giddy; expectation whirls me round'. That self-involved, apprehensive 'I' who was giddily whirled is now absorbed into the sense of felt mutuality in 'us', 'our lips', 'we two', which permeates this entire speech, affirming the reality of 'our' joined lives which chance now separates. It is a mark of Troilus' integrity and his depth that he is capable of such an experience of strain and conflict (Paris, for example, seems by contrast a shallower man, more lightweight, incapable of this degree of pain, longing and resilience). And equally it is a mark of this *play's* distinctive greatness: for Shakespeare here succeeds in expressing Troilus' desire and frustration so compellingly that the audience can imaginatively apprehend the inward reality of his turmoil at the same time as it observes it more dispassionately from the outside.

The final passage in the scene, as the time closes in when Troilus must hand Cressida over to Diomedes, is also rendered with great economy and power. Amidst the larger group now gathered for her 'interchange', the familiar trio of Troilus, Pandarus and Cressida is suddenly 'changed' and replaced by a new triangle. The stage-grouping here as elsewhere makes its own sharp point. Cressida's silence as she stands with Troilus and Diomedes recalls and starkly contrasts with her blushing silence in Act III Scene ii when her uncle jovially handed her to Troilus, saying 'Here she is now'; and here, as there, Troilus' agitation resembles hers, though he summons his best gallantry: 'Welcome, Sir Diomed! Here is the lady ...'. Again, Shakespeare's double entendres gratingly accentuate the ironies of Troilus' courtesy towards this sleek Greek:

> At the port, lord, I'll give her to thy hand,
> And by the way possess thee what she is.
>
> (IV.iv. 110–11)

He means of course that he will tell Diomedes about her so as to safeguard her against any ill-treatment, but his words unwittingly highlight all the slipperiness of 'possession' that is so central to the play's exploration of love and war, both in these three's relationships and in others as well, especially those of the analogous triangle of Menelaus, Helen and Paris. In what senses does Troilus 'possess' Cressida (or not possess her), and stand to lose her? Who can be sure exactly 'what she is' and what she is not? In what ways does Cressida 'possess' herself or (in both senses) own what she is, or belong to another? What does it mean for a person to be possessed of another, or dispossessed? Patently (and not least to Diomedes) this Troilus who must 'give her' away, desires to have and to keep her as his own (and his alone); but it is striking here how this desire immediately rouses Diomedes' will to have her as *his* 'mistress', as he puts it, for he pointedly ignores Troilus, turns straight to Cressida, and stakes his claim.

Thus, as with Helen, so with Cressida, the likelihood of

violent conflict over the question of whose she is arises here
even before she leaves the stronghold of Troy, as Troilus
flares in retaliation against Diomedes' appropriative
insolence, and his conditional promise of safety for
Diomedes is suddenly changed to a conditional threat, 'if ...
not ... I'll cut thy throat'. Diomedes' closing couplet
contemptuously repudiates Troilus' will in terms that serve
to epitomise all those clashes of desire and limit that fill
these central scenes, when he says, '... But that you say,
"Be't so",/I speak it in my spirit and honour, "No".' And in
a rich variety of forms, this sort of flat contradiction
between contrary facts or oppugnant wills— *'Be't so'*: *'No'*—
remains the central focus of the drama right to the end.

· 4 ·

'Changeful potency'

'Without contraries is no progression', Blake wrote; but despite the revolutionary optimism that implies, the Trojan War as imaged in the first four Acts of *Troilus* shows conflict issuing in stalemate, frustration and inertia, rather than in 'progress'; and in considering how the play itself 'develops' as it moves towards its close it needs to be asked whether the contrary energies of the drama here work to forge any new realisation of human potentialities, or whether the play's habitual mode of discoursing 'with and against itself' issues only in a somewhat sterile, inconclusive or negative clash of ideas. What, if any, valuable awareness of human nature is born of this quarrel-riddled and quarrel-engendering play? What is the *thrust* of the drama, what activity of mind and imagination do its closing Acts express and excite? And—to put it in a broader context—how does *Troilus* relate to and compare with others of Shakespeare's plays? Is it one of his great creative achievements, or is it rather a 'negative', self-negating, even nihilistic play?

Remembering its 'changeful potency' earlier on—especially its sudden shifts of pace, direction and mood—one naturally anticipates further changes to come, though quite what these will involve is unpredictable, anyone's guess—and everyone seems to be guessing incessantly, ourselves as well. As at every moment the mind turns back

in retrospect of what has passed, so it casts forward to the
prospect of what lies still pent in the word 'hereafter'.

In the Trojan council Hector had said:

> There is no lady of more softer bowels,
> More spongy to suck in the sense of fear,
> More ready to cry out 'Who knows what follows?'
> Than Hector is.
>
> > (II.ii. 11–14)

Later in the play there is still no certain answer to that
question, 'What follows?', and hence Greeks and Trojans
alike, projecting their expectation out of their loves and
hates, desires and fears, convince themselves that they know
exactly what the outcome will be. Shakespeare takes it for
granted that the audience does in a general way know 'what
follows'—that Cressida will be untrue, that Hector will be
killed, Troy destroyed. Yet as the play moves towards the
fulfilment of these expectations it keeps dropping hints and
cautions of the need to reserve some 'modest doubt' not
only about the specific facts of what may happen, but about
exactly what their value and significance will be. When
Hector at the end of Act II Scene iii ignores his own warning
of the perils of over-confidence we may (in Nestor's phrase)
find Shakespeare's 'purpose/Pointing on' *us*, defying us to
ignore the risks of 'surety secure' in our knowledge of what
follows.

Nor is Hector's by any means the only such tacit challenge
to vigilance. The characters' habitual self-consciousness
does nothing to prevent their equally habitual self-unseeing;
and this, along with their frequent references to 'glasses',
mirrors and self-images, and their frequent adverse
judgements of each other and flattering images of
themselves, makes the play seem in certain respects to
anticipate Swift's remark that 'Satire is a sort of glass,
wherein beholders do generally discover everybody's face
but their own'. If so, the universality of much of its language

may further needle us to wonder how far the point applies to
us, the spectators, as well as to these Trojans and Greeks,
one of whom, Achilles, sweepingly remarks that

> speculation turns not to itself
> Till it hath travell'd, and is mirror'd there
> Where it may see itself.
>
> (III.iii. 109–11)

At the outset the Prologue had said, speaking of the
Greeks and Trojans, 'Now expectation ... /On one and
other side,... /Sets all on hazard'; and by Act IV that link
between 'expectation' and 'hazard' has been underlined
time and again, not merely by the frequent jolting of the
characters' expectations but by the frequent similar jolting
of our own. Our experience as we watch seems in this way
analogous to theirs: we too keep expecting what we do not
get, and getting what we don't expect. Whatever the case in
other plays, the privileges afforded to this one's audience
evidently don't include immunity from the hazards of
expectancy that beset its protagonists. Just as their wishes
are often disappointed, their conjectures unmet, their
confidence betrayed, a similar fate can await our own
'supposes' and presumptions; and it seems unwise to ignore
the chance (in Agamemnon's words) of something even yet
going 'tortive and errant', 'bias and thwart',

> not answering the aim,
> And that unbodied figure of the thought
> That gave't surmised shape.
>
> (I.iii. 15–17)

Early in the play, we were tipped off to heed the way
minor events can prefigure major ones, when Nestor
remarked how

in such indexes, although small pricks
To their subsequent volumes, there is seen
The baby figure of the giant mass
Of things to come at large.

                                        (I.iii. 343–6)

Nestor's optimism there about Ulysses' 'project'—'I begin
to relish thy advice;/And I will give a taste thereof
forthwith/To Agamemnon'—had reinforced Ulysses' own
already sharp 'imaginary relish' at the delicious success of
his plan to 'pluck down Achilles' plumes' by glorifying Ajax
(making *him* heroically answer Hector's challenge instead of
Achilles). But the elaborate scheme only comes to fruition
late in Act IV, when the by now grotesquely swollen-egoed
Ajax ('prophetically proud of an heroical cudgelling', as
Thersites says) bombastically bids the trumpeter 'crack thy
lungs', 'split thy ... pipe', 'stretch thy chest, and let thy eyes
spout blood' in blowing for Hector: a *tremendous*
summoning blast, to which the response is—nothing! 'No
trumpet answers', mutters the baffled Ulysses. And this
great bathos of things 'not answering' does seem to serve
as an 'index' of 'what follows' when Hector eventually
arrives, for the grand contest everyone has been expecting
since Act I, staged with much of the palaver of the
Bolingbroke/Mowbray contest in *Richard II* is, like that one,
abruptly aborted. Hector calls it off, much to Ajax's chagrin:

Aeneas	There is expectance here from both the sides
	What further you will do.
Hector	We'll answer it:
	The issue is embracement. Ajax, farewell.

                                        (IV.v. 146–8)

This great flop of Ulysses' great scheme is on Shakespeare's
part a superbly managed anti-climax; and one of its
functions in 'not answering' the 'unbodied figure' of

everyone's surmises is precisely to raise new surmises and expectations about what's 'yet in the word "hereafter"' (cf. I.i. 22ff).

The early and middle stretches of the play are crowded with small 'indexes' of 'things to come at large', 'baby figures' of Cressida's frailty, and—echoing Cassandra's prophecy—countless intimations of disaster in the war: as when Ulysses pictures Ajax being congratulated 'As if his foot were on brave Hector's breast,/And great Troy shrinking' or shrieking—'shriking', as the Quarto has it (III.iii. 140–1). During Act IV these intensify, and so does the sense of exposure 'to dangers/As infinite as imminent' (IV.iii. 67–8), as Cressida's impending fall is insistently associated with the fall of Hector and of Troy. Both events are strikingly prefigured in this same scene which includes the duel with Ajax (IV.v). The trumpet-blast summoning Hector is answered, not by the expected arrival of the armoured hero, but by the silent approach of an unarmed woman who is soon denounced as a strumpet: into the arena walks Cressida, squired by the redoubtable Diomedes, and is promptly embraced and kissed by all the Greek generals in turn. It is a startling event, and distressing too in what it portends for her and for Troilus. But although it is easy to be mesmerised by this outbreak of general kissing, one cannot when actually watching the play ignore the parallel with its sequel: in this same scene, the fiasco of the 'sportful combat' with Ajax issues in another and equally unexpected 'loving interview', when Hector is greeted and embraced by all the Greek generals in turn.

This remarkable scene (IV.v), with its duo of 'interviews' sandwiching the no less extraordinary inconclusive tournament, is one of Shakespeare's most original inventions in the play, and both in the details of its component parts and in its strange tripartite construction, merits closer attention than it usually gets.

(i)

In critical discussions and stage renditions of Cressida's 'arrival' here, it is often assumed that Ulysses' castigation of her at the end of the business serves as a retrospective stage direction, a clear injunction from Shakespeare as to how the incident should be played:

> Fie, fie upon her!
> There's language in her eye, her cheek, her lip,
> Nay, her foot speaks; her wanton spirits look out
> At every joint and motive of her body.
>
> (IV.v. 54–7)

Of course, it is possible and indeed very common to have Cressida appearing in this scene as every bit the come-hitherish tart that Ulysses takes her to be; but the script in fact gives good reason to judge that Ulysses' judgement is hardly impartial, hardly (in Agamemnon's terms) 'strain'd purely from all hollow bias-drawing'. Indeed, his reaction to Cressida and his generalised denunciation of 'these encounterers', these 'sluttish spoils of opportunity,/And daughters of the game', can be seen to reveal rather more about his own moral psychology than about this young woman just arrived from Troy. (His hostile sexual consciousness again seems interestingly akin to that of the repressed and repressive Angelo in *Measure for Measure*.)

The play's only previous indication of Ulysses' attitude to a woman was in Act III Scene iii, when he disclosed to Achilles his knowledge that 'you are in love/With one of Priam's daughters'—an affair he claims to know all about, as 'perfectly' as Achilles himself—when he pictures the man's sexual relations with the woman as a type of violent conquest, analogous to, but less worthy than, slaying the enemy: 'better would it fit Achilles much/To throw down Hector than Polyxena'. (So much for being 'in love'.) In the arrival scene it seems pretty clear that better would it suit

Ulysses much if the Greeks had kept the captive Antenor instead of trading him for this female who is clearly such a poor exchange from the military point of view. Things are not going well for Ulysses at this moment, what with the last-minute hitch in his carefully stage-managed promotion of Ajax; and when Agamemnon spots the approaching twosome—'Is not yond Diomed, with Calchas' daughter?'—Ulysses ignores the woman and remarks only on the man (Diomedes, 'rising on the toe', is evidently pleased with the figure he cuts with Cressida by his side). But the most striking thing is Ulysses' reaction when Agamemnon greets her. Upon old Nestor's well-meaning explanation, 'Our general doth salute you with a kiss' (in case she's in some doubt!), he cannot resist a cutting witticism: 'Yet is the kindness but particular;/'Twere better she were kiss'd in general'.

It was an inspired stroke on Shakespeare's part to have Ulysses thus be the one who proposes the general kissing for which he will then stigmatise the woman as a common whore. Even in these first few moments after her arrival Ulysses' repugnance or at best disdain can be felt in his coldly distancing use of the third person—'she'—in contrast with the others' style of addressing her directly as 'sweet lady','you', 'fair lady'. ''Twere better she were kissed in general'? Better for whom?

Cressida remains silent while they all take their kisses: Agamemnon, Nestor, Achilles, Patroclus (twice) until it comes once more to the self-deprecating Menelaus' turn— and he is the first to ask her leave—a silence during which her bodily language may express nothing remotely like the free invitation that Ulysses later claims he could read even in 'her foot'. Achilles' remark, 'I'll take that winter from your lips, fair lady', indicates that at that stage at least her manner is more coldly impassive, frozen, than warmly receptive— unless of course (unusually for him) he is being sarcastic in this. Achilles' comment also underlines the fact that, for Cressida, being 'kissed in general' means being kissed in

particular, by a series of particular and very different men
who enjoy it severally as well as jointly. Achilles' lips, then
Patroclus', no doubt take what they want from hers more
relishingly, more rapaciously, than do Nestor's or
Agamemnon's; but while, throughout all of this, Cressida
does not say a word, our attention is strongly drawn to what,
subjectively, it means for her to be the object of these
pleasure-takings. Notably, when she does at last speak she
uses her 'quick sense', her wit, not to solicit kisses but to
fend them off. What's more, she succeeds. With Menelaus,
as he himself admits, 'you fillip me o' th' head'; and with
Ulysses—according to the Quarto text—she delivers a
superb snub to his expressed desire for a kiss: 'Why begge
then'. Why—*beg* then: the cool stress on 'beg' is a knockout.
Later editions have emended this to something more
playfully acquiescent, on the Ulysses-inspired assumption
that Cressida displays an 'oncoming disposition' thoughout
this whole exchange. Most recently, for instance, the Arden
edition (1982) follows Johnson's conjecture, 'Why, beg
two', on these grounds, and the Oxford edition (1982)
accepts another conjecture, 'Why, beg too', claiming that
this is 'an obvious improvement' since Cressida's 'banter
with the Greeks' is in rhymed verse. But the Quarto's *jolt*
from the rhyme is the verbal equivalent as well as the means
of Cressida's jolting of Ulysses' expectation—a jolt
precisely gauged to declare that her 'desire' does not chime
with his, and which, in so successfully refusing his kiss,
thereby clearly piques him, as his retaliatory snubs make
plain. If this is so, then the mismatch is patent between
Cressida's pointed rebuff and Ulysses' nettled description
of her as one of those whorish 'encounterers' that 'give a
coasting welcome ere it comes'. When was a welcome so like
a spit in the eye?

Such evidences of friction and hence of fiction in Ulysses'
reaction to Cressida which cross-bias the little drama of this
arrival scene make it both more subtly pointed and more
poignant than if his outburst—'fie upon her!'—simply

squares with what we see. Indeed, in productions where Cressida does come on here as an eager-eyed coquette signalling her availability to all and sundry, much of the tension is thereby lost from her next scene when she dallies with Diomedes and lets herself be won. Rather than being in effect a repeat performance of a wantonness already displayed fully fledged in the 'arrival' scene, that scene with Diomedes in Act V marks a crucial change in her: the collapse of her vow to Troilus the minute she 'tempt[s] the frailty of [her] powers'. In the earlier of the two scenes the chance of such a collapse is as prominent in her own mind as in Diomedes' and in ours (signalled in her by defensiveness, in him by complacent standing-by); but this, her first encounter with the Greeks, does not settle the matter. Instead, it highlights the crucial *questions* of what will become of her and what she will become "'mongst the merry Greeks', who already treat her as a whore. Rather than exposing her as a stereotypical 'encounterer', the play exposes the self-confirming bent of a stereotyping mentality such as Ulysses'; his penchant for moral generalities (especially those that degrade other people and so confirm his superior position in the moral-political hierarchy) is acutely scrutinised, not obtusely 'approved', by the play.

The basic point at issue here—of what the 'arrival' incident shows—is obviously less important in the play as a whole than is the later scene with Diomedes, but it is not unimportant: it reveals that here as elsewhere the play's conception of Cressida and of her situation is more finely tuned and more comprehensive than that of any of the men it shows her now and henceforth surrounded by. And the carefully established dramatic context of the incident confirms that it marks the possibility of her becoming changed rather than the virtual completion of the change— and so too does its location, the physical and symbolic site where it takes place. For it occurs in the very arena marked out for the duel that is expected to determine the superior strength either of Ajax or of Hector, but whose outcome is suspended—no decisive conclusion is reached.

As was made clear when the challenge was proclaimed, this all takes place, in the open space, *'mid-way between* [the Greeks'] tents and walls of Troy' (I.iii. 278): in the middle territory, the no-man's land, the meeting-place and battle-ground of the two opposing sides. No longer is Cressida now in the protected zone of 'yon city', safe inside its 'strong immures' and its great gates with their 'massy staples/And corresponsive and fulfilling bolts' (Prologue, 17–18), but neither is she as yet arrived in the camp of the Greeks. She is out in the precarious open, halfway between her heart's home and that strange unknown but feared destination. The duel that will take place within her between her love for Troilus and her attraction to Diomedes has not yet been waged 'to the uttermost', and the issue remains suspended here—Diomedes has yet neither lost nor won.

In this 'mid-way' siting, together with all the verbal, physical and moral-psychological details of the incident, the scene presents a variety of 'indexes' to the possible 'subsequent volume' of Cressida's future in the Greek camp. Despite the pressures on her here of being the sole woman in a ring of strangers all bent on kissing her, she does manage to hold her own against the attentions and intentions of some; and this fact is significant—but not because the play is paving a way for the audience to regard her infidelity to Troilus as morally unavoidable or simply thrust upon her (for that is not what the later betrayal scene shows), still less because the play is suggesting that 'under the circumstances, any woman would have fallen likewise'—though this argument is sometimes advanced in defence of Cressida (it happens also to be Thersites' line in condemning her and the female sex in general). Rather, its significance lies in its making clear both how much and how little her fate now depends on the 'kind of self' she will manage to be. Her witty aloofness here in warding off unwanted kisses shows her guarded self-possession, her strength in self-withholding, but the incident also shows just how insecure this is. The silent presence of Diomedes throughout the whole business serves as a constant visual reminder of how exposed she now is to her 'guardian' who (in her presence) had so derisively declared his intentions to Troilus in the previous scene:

> when I am hence
> I'll answer to my lust. And know you, lord,
> I'll nothing do on charge: to her own worth
> She shall be priz'd.

Now, as Diomedes escorts her away, his very walk ('rising on the toe') expresses something of that same arrogance, but it is Cressida's bearing, 'the manner of [her] gait', not Diomedes', that Ulysses remarks on now, perusing her with dislike-sharpened eyes rather as Achilles later eyes Hector, 'joint by joint': 'her wanton spirits look out/At every joint and motive of her body'. But an actress well fitted to the role need exaggerate nothing of this: simply by *being* the woman she is, young and beautiful, Cressida is very noticeably attractive, and not less so when her manner is standoffish rather than welcoming—as Troilus had found at the start, of course, almost fainting in the remembrance of 'her eyes, her hair, her cheek, her gait, her voice'. 'There's language in her eye, her cheek, her lip,/Nay, her foot speaks', says Ulysses, incensed. But the play here as elsewhere realises the ambiguity of all such 'language', and alerts us to the very distinction Ulysses collapses, between attractiveness and attractingness, between a woman being a woman (not 'mannish') and a woman being a flirt. In Act IV Scene iv, for instance, when Diomedes declared his rivalry to Troilus by reading out loud the 'language' of Cressida's face—'The lustre in your eye, heaven in your cheek,/Pleads your fair usage'—who would infer from this that Cressida has dried her tears and begun to ogle Diomedes? The fact that different witnesses will make different 'readings'—different valuations—of the same face or person or situation is as obvious within the play as it is amongst its critics or spectators. But whatever invitations or susceptibilities may be read in Cressida's face and 'gait' here as she walks off with the man whom we know intends to 'answer to [his] lust', Diomedes' saying 'I'll bring you to your father' sounds indeed ominous, the more so when we remember her reply to Pandarus' saying 'you must to your father':

> I will not, uncle. I have forgot my father;
> I know no touch of consanguinity,
> No kin, no love, no blood, no soul so near me
> As the sweet Troilus!
>
> (IV.v. 95–8)

For her muteness now as she is led off indicates that Diomedes will meet little or no resistance in bringing her in every sense 'to [her] father': from now on, the Greeks will not only identify her as (and thus help turn her into) a natural 'daughter of the game', but as Calchas' daughter, the nearest kin of 'the traitor' who betrayed his old allegiance to Troy. But the question is left open here as to whether the blood in her veins will prove thicker than the water in the fountain of her love for Troilus.

(ii)

It is clearly no accident therefore that this matter of 'consanguinity', blood-relatedness, is made so strangely salient in what immediately follows, when the Trojan troop arrives for the long-expected armed contest. Hector's challenge, as Ulysses had said, 'Relates in purpose only to Achilles' (I.iii. 323); and now, faced with Ajax instead, he declines to pursue the duel 'to the edge of all extremity' on the grounds that Ajax is his cousin. As Aeneas puts it:

This Ajax is half made of Hector's blood;
In love whereof half Hector stays at home;
Half heart, half hand, half Hector comes to seek
This blended knight, half Troyan and half Greek.
(IV.v. 83–6)

And in case anyone wasn't listening, Agamemnon repeats:

The combatants being kin
Half stints their strife before their strokes begin.
(IV.v. 92–3)

Coming from a poet who can do so much better if he
bothers to, such heavily alliterated jingly rhymed semi-
doggerel and the hammering away on 'half' as in a Liza
Doolittle exercise, may raise suspicions that Shakespeare
here has only half heart, half hand, half mind on the job. But
if (as Aeneas bids) we 'weigh him well','that which looks
like' nodding is actually a wink: a long wink, of the
embarassing sort that is all the harder to interpret because it
seems part of an intelligence test which the winker enjoys
watching people fail. Yet whatever degree of jest is involved,
this business of the half-hearted Hector and his cousin the
'blended knight' Ajax is more than merely whimsical and
not just incidental to the play's main concerns.

That Shakespeare had it in mind all along to make an issue
of their kinship is suggested by the prominence given it by
Alexander's introduction of Ajax in Act I Scene ii: 'there is
among the Greeks/A lord of Troyan blood, nephew to
Hector'. Significantly, Hector was there described as
enraged and hell-bent on wreaking havoc without stint, to
avenge Ajax's having 'yesterday' 'cop'd [him] in the battle
and struck him down'—which makes all the more
unexpected his insistence now on staying 'half at home'
because Ajax is half Trojan, and his exalted wish to avoid
draining 'any drop thou borrow'dst from thy mother,/My
sacred aunt'. Hector's family sentiment is thus nicely

undercut, for it appears that 'the obligation of our blood forbids/A gory emulation 'twixt us twain' only when this suits his mood and convenience. Ajax himself, who regards such scruples as 'too gentle and too free', is clearly unconstrained by any such 'obligation': 'I came to kill thee, cousin'.

Hector's bombastic language here (especially in his self-advertising brag about 'Neoptolemus so mirable') shows his egoistic zest for all this highly public commotion. Yet beyond the deflation of Hector's inflations Shakespeare appears to be thinking seriously here, as throughout the play, about 'the touch of consanguinity' and about what 'obligations of [their] blood' may (or may not) constrain people to choose to 'embrace' each other, and to acknowledge the bonds between them, rather than choosing to deny their kinship or affinity, to attack each other and even to kill.

Hector's particular point here has other general implications too. He insists that the 'commixtion' of blood in Ajax's veins makes it impossible to separate out or even to distinguish what is Grecian in him from what is Trojan: since people are not like heraldic emblems with a neat dividing line between right and left, dexter and sinister, no part of Ajax can be singled out as purely Greek or purely Trojan. Nothing in him is 'unmingled'. What makes him 'distinct' from Hector—other, alien, Greekish—is inextricably mixed with what makes them 'affin'd and kin'. It is therefore impossible to destroy the enemy without destroying the kinsman as well; indeed, to kill Ajax would be in effect to kill something of himself. These implications of Hector's argument are not made so explicit in this scene as they are in Shakespeare's previous history plays concerned with bloody civil wars, nor is *Troilus* so much concerned to test them 'to the edge of all extremity' as is the case in *King Lear*, written a few years later: 'But yet thou art my flesh, my blood, my daughter;/Or rather a disease that's in my flesh,/Which I must needs call mine; thou art a boil/

... /In my corrupted blood' (*King Lear*, II.iv. 220–4). Yet *Troilus* clearly points towards the Tragedies in this, especially in Act V. And although Ulysses is at his most cynical when he says in Act III Scene iii that 'one touch of nature makes the whole world kin', the play itself not cynically but sceptically weighs well some of the implications of that extended metaphor, in which *all* members of humankind are naturally kindred beings. Violent aggression between such 'kin' is violently self-destructive, and indeed (as suggested later in IV.v) Hector's murderous intents and acts will thus prove suicidal—a connection Shakespeare discovered to be crucial in such later tragedies as *Othello* and *Macbeth*.

Here in Act IV Scene v, however, Hector declares that 'the issue is embracement'; and as in the welcoming of Cressida so now in the duel and its aftermath of Hector's 'welcoming' by the Greeks, the play presents, amongst other possibilities, the image of an amicable, harmonious outcome of the war—a quite unexpected *comic* resolution to all the protracted and costly quarrel. Choreographically, so to speak, the gestures of 'embracing' repeated again and again during this scene serve in part to denote the possibility of reconciliation, *pax*, acceptance: the end of hostilities, bloodshed and deadlock, in happy union, good fellowship, 'loving' accord. But as with the Cressida incident, so here, as the Greeks embrace Hector,the gestic language of amity serves to aggravate and expose the animosities that underlie it. It seems that the spirit of enmity in man is the spirit of friendship in its converse mode—the one can easily transform into the other, each is always latent in the other.

This exchange of courtesies between mortal enemies is patterned after previous encounters between the 'noble foes' in moments of 'gentle truce'; but each time, and most of all here, everyone is conscious of the frailty and temporariness of the truce, because everyone is aware of the suppressed violence, the menacing energies that surge beneath the surface of this 'humane gentleness' (cf. IV.i.

7–34). Nowhere is the sheer precariousness of men's sociabilities more grimly apparent.

For here, as Hector fraternises with the Greeks, they all speak of their mutual intent to 'convive' 'tonight' and destroy each other 'tomorrow'. At the end of the reception-line waiting to 'welcome' Hector is Achilles. It is an ugly encounter, chillingly unlike the meeting and mutual admiration of those two other great Shakespearian rivals in a later play, Coriolanus and Aufidius, or even of Hal and Hotspur in the earlier *Henry IV, Part One*. For as these two feast their eyes on each other, 'quot[ing] joint by joint', nothing masks or glamorises their absolute oppugnancy. Only the tenuous truce holds back their will to kill.

(iii)

The closing moments of Act IV thus furnish 'as in way of taste', pungent samples of 'what's to come': as to the lovers, nothing bodes well, and as to the Trojans, nothing does either. On the one hand, now, according to Ulysses, Diomedes 'gives all gaze and bent of amorous view/On the fair Cressid', and although Troilus reassures himself that 'she was belov'd, she loved; she is, and doth', the dismal thought arises: 'But still sweet love is food for fortune's tooth'. And on the other hand, the signs are plain that if anyone's foot will end up on 'brave Hector's breast', it won't be Ajax's but that of Hector's real co-rival, the 'great hulk' Achilles. The temporary truce, like all such, is a provisional agreement, without guarantees, a convention requiring trust on both sides; and both sides here agree to stick to it only because it will end on the morrow:

> To-morrow do I meet thee, fell as death;
> To-night, all friends.

(IV.v. 268–9)

In Act I, determined to humble Achilles, Ulysses had said, 'Do not consent/That ever Hector and Achilles meet'; and since then that imperative has hung upon our minds, a covert warning of what may happen if dare-devil Hector ever 'wakes' the devil 'to answer'. Achilles lolling on his lazy bed the livelong day may have seemed rather ludicrous; but the idea looms of the extreme danger once Hector 'rouses' this dozing 'dog', who is also known as a 'sleeping giant'.

But how has this happened? Since the play began Achilles has had no intention whatsoever of challenging Hector, or anyone else. Shakespeare strikingly omits to provide the Homeric 'explanation' of this withdrawal, the bitter quarrel between Agamemnon and Achilles with which *The Iliad* opens. Instead, and deliberately it seems, we are left in the dark, or at best the half-light, about 'the cause' of his angry refusal; Ulysses' diagnosis of 'pride' points to a symptom, hardly the root cause, and nor do the various 'explanations' casually divulged late in the piece in Act III Scene iii solve the mystery (i.e. Achilles' love for the Trojan princess, Polyxena, and his love for Patroclus, who has 'little stomach to the war'), for these seem rather to conform with than to 'cause' his obdurate negative will. But all along, the baffling *fact* of his refusal has seemed absolute, unremovable, only made the more rigid by others' attempts to unfix it: 'I'll speak with nobody'; 'you know my mind, I'll fight no more 'gainst Troy'. Even Ulysses' goadings have stirred no appetite for blood, but instead,

> a woman's longing,
> An appetite that I am sick withal,
> To see great Hector in his weeds of peace;
> To talk with him, and to behold his visage,
> Even to my full of view.
>
> (III.iii. 237–41)

But the sight of Hector unarmed has suddenly changed this 'woman's longing' into something no censurer could term 'womanish', 'effeminate' (cf. I.i. 105–6; III.iii. 217–18):

> Tell me, ye heavens, in which part of his body
> Shall I destroy him? Whether there, or there, or there?
>
> (IV.v. 242–3)

There is now no question in Achilles' mind about whether
or not he will kill Hector; the only question is *where*; and his
imagination lunges further, to turn even this prospective
future 'shall' into a presumptive past-tense fact, as he
envisages 'the very breach whereout/Hector's great spirit
flew'.

This instantaneous and appalling change in Achilles,
whereby 'I'll fight no more' becomes this 'I shall' of
murderous intensity, seems as uncalculated on Achilles'
part as it is surely calculated on Shakespeare's. As with
Hector's own spontaneous switch from no to yes in the
council, it exposes the terrifying irrationality of such
impulsions and desires. Achilles' 'will' here seems
involuntary or prevoluntary. It rears up from some
primitive substratum of his self, from somewhere way
below the roots of 'reasons'. He wants to destroy Hector
because the prospect of doing so is irresistibly desirable. He
has a sudden 'stomach' or hunger for these meaty limbs.
None other will satisfy.

In disclosing *this* appetite and the way it rouses a like one
in Hector ('I'll kill thee everywhere, yea, o'er and o'er') the
play clearly reveals these two as kindred spirits in this—
however unlike they are in other ways. And it no less clearly
indicates that for any progress to be made when they meet in
'mere (i.e. absolute) oppugnancy' its cost will be the
extermination of one or both by the other. But as well as
foreshadowing this, their encounter here also (to anticipate
for a moment) precludes any over-sentimentalising
simplification on our part of Achilles' later actions, when
the death of Patroclus mobilises him to act on the 'longing'
already voiced here. This lust to kill *precedes* its vengeful
motive or immediate 'cause'. When, later, we hear that
'Patroclus' wounds have rous'd his drowsy blood', the

implication—prepared for in Act IV Scene v—is that Achilles' aggression had been temporarily torpid, needing only to be *woken*: till now, these latent energies have been held suspended, pent in his tent, as if simply waiting to be vented, let loose. Nor, in Act IV Scene v, is it possible to 'explain' Achilles' violence by saying that Hector 'causes' it or even 'provokes it', for it gathers and erupts within seconds of their coming face to face. The violence is there already, inside Achilles (and inside Hector), and while Hector's living flesh is here its target and the occasion of its bursting forth in words, its origin lies within Achilles' nature. It is part of his constitution, a bloodlust as native to him as the blood in his own veins.

Here, in Act IV Scene v, though, the truce requires that Achilles restrain this hunger until 'tomorrow'. But on the morrow—the next scene—all is again sent 'bias and thwart' when the war-like chariot of his desires meets the roadblock of Queen Hecuba's letter, and lurches round in yet another U-turn—'and suddenly': Queen Hecuba sends

> A token from her daughter, my fair love,
> Both taxing me and gaging me to keep
> An oath that I have sworn. I will not break it.
> Fall Greeks; fail fame; honour or go or stay;
> My major vow lies here, this I'll obey.
>
> (V.i. 38–42)

'An oath of faith that *I have sworn*': having just witnessed Achilles' savage threats to Hector (presumably after he had sworn this oath), we can hardly fail to realise how readily his will to 'break' his oath can overmaster his will to 'keep' it, for there no tender sense of 'obligation' to 'my fair love' had forbidden or checked a 'gory emulation' between Achilles and his 'fair love's' brother.

Although Achilles' love of Polyxena is peripheral to the main action, the fact of it is a significant donnée in the play. In modern productions, however, it has often been treated as much less important than other possibilities touched on in the portrait of Achilles. The modern trend of treating as gospel Thersites' remark about Patroclus being Achilles' 'masculine whore' has become pretty much *de rigueur* in major productions in England since the 1960s, and has sometimes involved the super-addition of much distracting stage business in productions bent on giving a high profile to high camp life in the Greek camp. (In the BBC television version, for example, Thersites appears in drag as a washerwoman, as if his obsession with filth and disease signalled a deeper lust for cleanliness; and other productions have gone further, with Thersites not as a queen, but more dizzyingly, played by a woman.) But the play does not deal in unexamined clichés, and the effect of such interpolations can be to make it rather *less* incisive than it actually is in its analysis of these various lives and relationships. When Thersites sneers, 'thou art said to be Achilles' male varlet', he clearly intends to insult and infuriate Patroclus; the charge is rather lame if its truth is patently obvious and indeed paraded whenever the two men appear.

(iv)

Achilles' 'major vow' and the questions of whether or for how long he will 'obey' it, or whether something in him will prove 'disobedient and refractory' even to himself, obviously links in our minds with, among others, Cressida and the 'oath of faith' that *she* has sworn. And as with her, so with Achilles, these spasmodic changes from 'I will not' to 'I will' to 'I will not' to 'I will', throw into even sharper prominence those basic questions about 'persistive constancy' and human self-consistency which the play has been engaged in pressing from the start.

In ushering Cressida to the gate (in IV.iv), shadowed by Diomedes, Troilus drew her arm into his, saying, 'To our own selves bend we our needful talk'; and in scene after scene the play itself has been drawing us likewise to bend our needful thought to their own selves—indeed, to question the very nature of human selfhood. In contrast to Aristotle's excursions in 'moral philosophy', for instance (to which there is a wittily anachronistic reference in Hector's lecture to his juniors in II.iii), Shakespeare's in this as in his other plays are much more open-ended and quizzically sceptical. There is no presumption in *Troilus* that identity is perspicuous, nor that it is ultimately explicable: it is more of a puzzle, a conundrum, something questionable and enigmatic, which the mind must circle round, wonderingly, anxiously, playfully, as best it can.

Thus, Troilus' yearning in the first scene, for example, 'Tell me, Apollo ... What Cressid is, what Pandar, and what we?', is later echoed parodically by the Greeks' catechism:

Achilles   ... Come, what's Agamemnon?
Thersites Thy commander, Achilles. Then tell me, Patroclus, what Achilles?
Patroclus Thy lord, Thersites. Then tell me, I pray thee, what's Thersites?
Thersites Thy knower, Patroclus. Then tell me, Patroclus, what art thou?
Patroclus Thou must tell that knowest.
Achilles   O, tell, tell!
Thersites I'll decline the whole question.

(II.iii. 40–9)

Clearly, these Greeks, like their creator—who seems in this scene to allude to himself as well as the great Creator (II.ii. 63)—get a lot of comic mileage out of all of this. Yet as even these two brief examples show, the dramatist's gamesome wit is also a mode of serious inquisition; and in fact its inquiry into the question, 'Do you know what a man is?' (I.ii. 243) reaches via the smile-provoking to the frown-provoking, and does so partly by stressing the nexus between 'smiles' and 'frowns'. The face or the self that beams is the same face that elsewhere lours; a frown is also a latent or potential smile, and vice versa; and it is just such *'changeful potency'* in people (to use Troilus' phrase) that the drama of so many scenes is centred upon, as in all the hobnobbing interludes between Greeks and Trojans (e.g. I.iii. 216–44; IV.i. 1–35; IV.iv. 108–36 and especially IV.v) where smiles of welcome and threats of malevolence co-exist and alternate, ferocity suspended in conviviality, treason in fair faith.

'Hector, whose patience/Is as a virtue fix'd, today was mov'd': so Alexander reports to Cressida in the second scene; and his phrase serves as a 'conduct' or 'guide' to what follows again and again, for as well as exposing the tendency in people to be 'stubborn', 'against all suit', the play spotlights this tendency of whatever is 'fixed' to 'move' or 'be moved'—for what 'is' to become severed from what 'was', for 'today's' desire to oust 'yesterday's' and be ousted in turn by 'tomorrow's'. From early on, major changes of mind and heart such as Hector's in the council have been mirrored in a host of minor ones; and the same applies even more in later stages of the play, where countless small examples of mercuriality likewise augment and generalise the significance of major ones like Achilles' and Cressida's. Throughout, the main dramatic focus is less on the 'causes' of such 'changefulness' ('what was his cause of anger?') than on the disorienting facts of it, and on its consequences ('what follows' from it) in individual lives, in personal relationships, in familial, social and political affairs.

Cressida's unwitting (and unwittingly clairvoyant) anxiety had centred on this in the scene of her first 'loving interview' with Troilus:

> I have a kind of self resides with you;
> But an unkind self that it self will leave
> To be another's fool. I would be gone.
> Where is my wit? I know not what I speak.
>
> (III.ii. 144–7)

—and her anxiety, given a new twist, reverberates in Troilus' own where he later begs her to 'be not tempted' by the cunning Grecians:

> Cressida   Do you think I will?
> Troilus   No,
>   But something may be done that we will not;
>   And sometimes we are devils to ourselves,
>   When we will tempt the frailty of our powers,
>   Presuming on their changeful potency.
>
>   (IV.iv. 91–6)

Like many of Troilus' speeches, this is hard to unravel simply, but its gist is clearly a caution against 'presuming on' or putting too much faith in our frail capacity to stay as we are, when in fact we are so perilously changeable, so liable to be traitorous 'devils to ourselves'. The 'changeful potency' of 'our powers' is (dismayingly) *theirs* rather than ours, apparently beyond our control, outside the province of our 'will'. To underrate this power of change is rashly to test, and prove, our frailty, our flimsy self-command. As Olivia says in *Twelfth Night*, 'ourselves we do not [own]'.

So conceived—and most of this play's characters are so conceived—a human self is no monolithic *entity* but more like an unaccountable *process*: strange, volatile, dividable, sometimes self-confounding, like Achilles when his pride 'quarrels at self-breath', 'batters down himself', 'entomb[s himself] alive'. And as such phrases indicate, the play's exploration of so many kinds of changefulness, inconsistency and self-conflict comprehends—in Act V above all—some much more disturbing possibilities than Shakespeare had envisaged in most of his plays to date (*Julius Caesar*, *Henry IV Part Two*, and *Hamlet* being major exceptions here). Many of his earlier plays are nevertheless clearly 'affin'd' to *Troilus* (and to the Sonnets) in being concerned to scrutinise the nature of personal identity, and even to question what sort of continuous existence it has, if any. But in *A Midsummer Night's Dream*, *Much Ado*, *As You Like It* and *Twelfth Night*, for instance—to mention only four such plays—the most lamentable comedies and painful scrapes resulting from all manner of inconstancy and fickleness can be happily enough resolved in the lovers' dance of 'faith and troth' at the close. Even the treacheries of *As You Like It* can be dissolved in instant 'conversions', evil malignity transformed into good will. If 'our powers' are shown to be 'frail' in the comedies, the 'devil' in the end comes hindmost. In contrast with that of any of those plays, the temper of *Troilus*—its glint, so to speak—in conceiving these unreliable selves, shares none of that moonshine gleam of the *Dream* and none of that subtly opalesque quality of *Twelfth Night*. The 'changeful potencies' imagined here—and especially in the last two Acts—are far less benign and harmless than any suggested by such terms as Feste's, for example, in speaking of Orsino's professed constancy:

> Now the melancholy god protect thee; and the tailor make thy doublet of changeable taffeta, for thy mind is a very opal.
>
> (*Twelfth Night*, II.iv. 72–4)

Troilus presents only a finite range of human selves, of course; but its range is not as narrow as some accounts of the play imply. It is arguably wider than in any previous English drama by Shakespeare or anyone else, for it includes such immensely different (and immensely changeful) modes of human being as those of Achilles and Troilus; Pandarus and Cassandra; Cressida and Thersites; Hector, Ajax, Agamemnon—and others no less memorably individualised, memorably diverse. The creation of such beings as Achilles and Cressida is magnificent—the latter, I think, going beyond the achievement of any of Shakespeare's previous conceptions of a woman in its subtlety and its bracing unideality. The Achilles likewise shows a high degree of originality in the way Shakespeare here again freely adds and subtracts, adopts and adapts, suggestions in his various source-materials to create an Achilles whose 'commixtion' of susceptibilities and aggressiveness commands attention throughout. Notably, Shakespeare strips away all the (very Elizabethan) ethical colouring that Chapman had given to *his* portrait of Achilles in his translation of *The Iliad*, seven books of which (1–2 and 7–11) had been published in 1598, where Achilles is translated into an exemplary hero, temperate, self-controlled and patriotic. Shakespeare's Achilles (like Homer's) is a much more complex moral phenomenon than Chapman's, presaging such other sometimes tender-hearted dragons as he was later to create in Macbeth and Coriolanus.

On the other hand, with an eye to the Tragedies and the late plays, it is arguable that the range of kinds of self explored in *Troilus* is more restrictive, and achieved at some cost. In particular, by concentrating so intensely on such *momentary* selves (i.e. selves for whom the passage of time consists in fragmentation, in the experience of disjunctive moments) the play seems deliberately to marginalise the possibility of other modes of living amidst time: the possibility of experiencing a strong continuity between what has been, is and will be, for instance, or of discovering one's present and future to be deep-rooted in one's past, or of discovering one's human nature to be shaped and changed by larger *impersonal* rhythms or forces in the greater Nature of its circumambient world. *Troilus* expresses a state of mind and a conception of human nature in which such possibilities of 'integrity' or wholeness over a span of time are almost unimaginable. The area of change it is interested in is the ceaseless fluctuations of people's hopes, desires, dreads, appetites. And while this concentration is the play's main strength, it may also be seen as limiting its scope somewhat in contrast to that of subsequent plays.

Similarly with the nature of the particular selves it includes. The conception of character is profound, but the

characters on the whole are not beings who experience the
world or themselves in a deep, inward, complex way, like
Hamlet or Macbeth or Leontes. Shakespeare here devotes
more energy to imagining and comparing a great variety of
changeful and/or dividable selves than to probing far into
their *interior* reality as he does in later plays. In the case of
Thersites, say, or Achilles or Pandarus, a quite considerable
inner life is dramatically implied; but most of the play's
other selves (Hector and Ulysses, for example) are imagined
as having little private inner life and even less self-awareness
of what goes on inside them. The outstanding exception
here of course is Troilus himself at various points, and to a
lesser extent, Cressida. In each of them, and especially in
Troilus in Acts IV and V, the drama creates with complete
convincingness the inward quiddity of a self acutely alive to
the multiple promptings of its innermost being—one who
(as Troilus puts it in V.ii) knows what it is to 'be myself' and
to 'have cognition/Of what I feel'. But for the most part, the
drama in *Troilus* is centred elsewhere, on the vast shifting
network of personal and political relationships between its
separate selves, rather than on the singular experiential
complexities of each, or of a central figure (or couple) who
dominates the action of the whole play. Thus it touches on
but does not plumb those regions of experience where
prayers cross (as for Macbeth, or Angelo in *Measure*); or
where a self knows the turmoil of finding itself
bewilderingly changeable and unfixed (as in those plays
again); or where (as for Antony) the sheer flux and
metamorphic fluidity of experience can seem to render
one's very self vapourish, cloud-like, dissoluble. In this
sense, the inquiry in *Troilus* into human selves ('Do you
know what a man *is*?') is focused differently and is perhaps
less penetrating and less profoundly analytic than that in any
of the Tragedies. It sharply raises but does not pursue 'to the
uttermost' those radical questions that galvanise the drama
of *King Lear*: 'Who is it that can tell me who I am?'; 'Is man
no more than this?', 'Is there any cause in nature that make

these hard hearts?'.

These later plays may suggest some of the outer limits of *Troilus'* achievement. But they also suggest how creatively adventurous it is too—as well as being (so hindsight shows) a watershed, and of seminal importance for all of Shakespeare's 'subsequent volumes'.

(v)

Although Cressida's betrayal of Troilus is foreshadowed so many times, our expectation of it does not ease the strain of watching it happen, nor do Troilus' own forebodings soften the unprotected shock of it for him. In Act III Scene ii he had stayed for Pandarus 'to conduct him thither' to Cressida, but now he asks Ulysses to act as his 'Charon', 'to bring me thither' where Cressida resides (significantly, at the cuckold Menelaus' tent); and as the two of them follow Diomedes' torch through the midnight camp, Thersites' voice is heard (by us) croaking out of the darkness:

> That same Diomed's a false-hearted rogue.... They say he keeps a Troyan drab, and uses the traitor Calchas' tent. I'll after. Nothing but lechery! All incontinent varlets!
> (V.i. 86, 93–5)

'They say': evidently the Ulyssean view of Cressida has already gone into circulation as the common currency. But however much or little we resist the idea of her as a kept 'drab', it is immediately confirmed by our first glimpse of her in the Greek camp: with her face pressed close to Diomedes' she whispers in his ear—a gesture whose intimacy dazes and appals Troilus as he watches from the shadows this spectacle lit up by the flare of his rival's torch.

In terms of its dramatic design this great scene (V.ii) is among the most brilliant and celebrated in the play, and indeed in all Shakespeare. Previously, he had already

proven himself a master-craftsman of 'eavesdropping'
scenes: in *Much Ado About Nothing*, for instance (II.iii, III.i,
III.iii and elsewhere) and *Twelfth Night* (the box-tree scene,
II.v, for example), as well as those in *Hamlet* including the
fatal one with Polonius behind the arras (III.iv); and soon
after completing *Troilus* he was to compose the remarkable
scene—strongly reminiscent of this one—in which Othello
witnesses what he takes as proof of Cassio's supposed affair
with Desdemona (IV.i). But the most elaborately structured
of all is this scene with Cressida and Diomedes watched and
overheard by Troilus, watched and overheard by Ulysses
and by Thersites—all watched and overheard by us. As
many commentators have well brought out, it is far easier to
get a sense of this on the stage than on the page. Visually,
everyone's attention centres on the illumined figures of
Cressida and Diomedes, whilst our notice, along with
Thersites', is equally caught by Troilus' reactions—he of
course being unaware of Thersites' gloating asides.

'Prince Troilus, I have lov'd you night and day/For many
weary months' (III.ii. 111): the play makes it no more
possible for us than for Troilus to forget that heart-whole
Cressida whose 'love' (as she said at their parting) 'admits no
qualifying dross', in watching now as she waveringly courts,
puts off, appeases, caresses and yields to Diomedes, now
drawn towards him and now drawn backward by half-
hearted misgivings, desires and regrets.

> *Diomedes* Will you remember?
> *Cressida*   Remember? Yes.
> *Diomedes* Nay, but do, then;
>   And let your mind be coupled with your
>   words.
> *Troilus*   What shall she remember?
>
> (V.ii. 12–16)

In this context Diomedes' phrase, 'be coupled', is hardly
leerless; no onlooker can fail to see that the coupling

proposed is not just of minds and words. The significance of that future coupling and this present conversation is dramatically 'coupled' to the past, and the reiteration of 'remember?', 'remember?', 'remember?', as the query slips from Diomedes' mind to Cressida's and finally to Troilus', underscores the grounds of Troilus' sheer dismay in witnessing here the withering of her remembrance of *him*. What his tortured memory cannot forget for an instant Cressida recalls only to let it slide from mind—'He lov'd me'—as she offers and then withholds from Diomedes the 'sleeve' which betokened Troilus' love, and fancies Troilus at home in Troy 'thinking ... of ... me' and giving 'memorial dainty kisses' to her love-token.

Repeatedly during the play we have watched people looking *at* others, observing from a distance that is as much psychological as spatial; but never till now has Cressida been dramatically presented at such a remove as she is here, where our view of her is physically and emotionally framed by the three on-stage watchers whose observations all impinge on ours, and where the continual rapid shifts from one speaker to another and another cause our attention to zig-zag, exacerbating that sense of consternation, of sudden estrangement from her, which the disconcerting visual tableau produces in our minds. Where Chaucer sorrowfully equivocates about her relations with 'this sodeyn Diomede', 'Men seyn—I not—that she [gave] hym hire herte' (*Troilus and Criseyde*, V. 841–1099ff), Shakespeare's conception is much more stark. 'I have abandon'd Troy, left my possessions,/Incurr'd a traitor's name, expos'd myself/... To doubtful fortunes': thus Calchas in Act III Scene iii; but his daughter following in his footsteps here has none of the force or definiteness expressed in those decisive verbs. She falters; and whilst her vacillations are a kind of shiftless self-treason, this conflux of yeas and nays, of 'Be't so'/'No', the shilly-shallying of a self surprised by its own infirmity of will, also give the scene its edge of pathetic and dismal *familiarity*. It is as if we—and she—recognise what is

happening, not as something wholly new or strange but as a
possibility already previously glimpsed as such and then
blocked out of mind. ('More dregs than water, if my fears
have eyes'.) The drama poignantly reveals her half-careless
self-abandonment in the way she relinquishes the sleeve
('He that takes that doth take my heart withal'), having
incited Diomedes to snatch it ('I had your heart before; this
follows it'), and sighs "tis done, 'tis past; and yet it is not;/I
will not keep my word'. In a speech reminiscent of Ulysses'
in Act III Scene iii. ('The present eye praises the present
object'), she wanly condemns her 'turpitude' in allowing her
mind to be swayed by her eyes, and in lukewarmly
farewelling Troilus and welcoming Diomedes (cf. Ulysses:
'the welcome ever smiles,/And farewell goes out sighing'),
she lets herself float adrift from all her yesterdays, and even
from today—the 'weary months' and the night and morrow
of love (this very day) which had succeeded them. And yet
she remains unmistakably Cressida—not a different person,
but the same, changed.

Earlier in this day, when she was met by the Greeks,
Agamemnon, the first to embrace her, had said on repeating
the gesture to Hector shortly afterwards:

> What's past and what's to come is strew'd with husks
> And formless ruin of oblivion;
> But in this extant moment, faith and troth,
> Strain'd purely from all hollow bias-drawing,
> Bids thee with most divine integrity,
> From heart of very heart, great Hector, welcome.
>
> (IV.v. 166–71)

What kind of 'integrity' is it in which the present moment is
thus disjoined from past and future, in which memory and
anticipation can thus be shed from mind? What kind of self
is it whose past and future can be mentally discarded,
ignored, neglected 'as if forgot'? What kind of world is it in

which continuity of meaning and value from one moment to the next is deemed worthless or denied?

The 'integrity' of *Troilus and Cressida* itself includes the pressure it constantly puts on questions such as these—as it does so memorably in this scene of Cressida's faithlessness by insisting both on the connections and the discontinuities between 'this extant moment' and 'what's past' and 'what's to come'. Far from strewing the past and future with husks and ruin of oblivion, the drama works to keep them powerfully in mind; the value and significance of each and every 'extant moment' is realised as consisting both in its unique particularity and in its indissoluble relationships with all those other particular heres and nows, thens and theres.

Thus, both visually and verbally the resemblances and contrasts between this wooing scene and previous moments (and later ones) are painfully marked. In Troilus and Cressida's own coming-together, for instance, Troilus, whirled by expectation, had wondered aloud 'what will it be/When that the wat'ry palate tastes indeed/Love's thrice-repured nectar?'; but now that dream of sweetness is smashed, and he reels from a quite other giddiness as he overhears her dalliance with her 'sweet guardian', her 'sweet honey Greek': 'I prithee, do not hold me to mine oath;/Bid me do anything but that, sweet Greek' (V.ii. 26–7). Thus, 'palating the taste of her dishonour' (cf. IV.i. 61), he finds it 'anything but' 'sweet'—only 'orts', 'fragments, scraps, the bits, and greasy relics/Of her o'er-eaten faith', tun'd too sharp in bitterness for the capacity of his ruder powers (cf. III.ii. 23–4). In the opening scene he had bewailed the pangs inflicted on 'the open ulcer of [his] heart', the heart which, 'As wedged with a sigh, would rive in twain': 'O gods, how do you plague me!'; 'Patience herself, what goddess e'er she be,/Doth lesser blench at suff'rance than I do'. But now in what (in Nestor's terms in I.iii) is a far more deadly 'storm of fortune' (worsened far by the memory of 'her ray and brightness') his 'hopes lie drown'd' utterly, 'made a toast for

Neptune', and he knows too well 'how many fathoms deep/They lie indrench'd': 'O plague and madness!'. He strives in vain to be patient—'I will be patient'; 'I am all patience'; 'I will be patient; outwardly I will'—but no 'guard of patience' can restrain his outbursting misery as Cressida's words and actions 'lay in every gash that love hath given me/The knife that made it' (cf. I.i. 61).

'You are moved, Prince; let us depart', says Ulysses, surprised alike by Troilus' passion and his naïvety, and worried because 'this place is dangerous;/The time right deadly'. And despite many critics' reluctance to be 'moved' in sympathy with Troilus, it is hard to imagine a good stage rendition which could leave the audience 'fixed', unmoved—and this notwithstanding that the scene includes Ulysses who is not much, and Thersites who is not at all, in sympathy with the young lover's grief. To Thersites, of course, nothing he now sees or hears is in the least surprising: Troilus is simply a stock comic figure in a familiar farce which confirms what Thersites knew already, that all 'love' is a species of lechery, human suffering completely absurd. He is immensely *gratified* by the spectacle of Cressida and Diomedes, which so entirely fits his expectations. His presence and his crowing relish are of great importance here; to undervalue their effect is greatly to weaken the power of the scene:

> How the devil luxuy, with his fat rump and potato finger, tickles these together! Fry, lechery, fry!
>
> (V.ii. 55–7)

Like Iago's obscene imaginings in *Othello*, this has an unforgettable graphic potency; yet as with Pandarus' prurience in Act III Scene ii, Thersites' lip-smacking sexual excitements are one element among others here, and to accord them overriding importance is to falsify the whole in which his exultant knowingness reveals him also to be grotesquely *un*knowing—ignorant of other kinds of experience which are here given no less cogent expression than his own.

Ulysses' presence and his reactions are important as well, partly because none of this has much personal significance for him: he neither greatly relishes it like Thersites, nor greatly suffers like Troilus. He refrains from moralistic censure or sage 'I could have told you so's', but he shows no imaginative capacity to grasp what it means for Troilus to have his heart 'wedged', 'riven in twain', 'blown up by th' root' (to use Pandarus' phrase; cf IV.iii. 53)—even though Ulysses was himself the man who in the sphere of his own (political) concerns had imaged a chaos in which cosmic commotions

> Divert and crack, rend and deracinate,
> The unity and married calm of states
> Quite from their fixture!
>
> (I.iii. 99–101)

Troilus' experience of this betrayal is indeed such a chaos—a 'chaos of thought and passion, all confused' (to use Pope's phrase from the *Essay on Man*)—in which his 'heart of very heart' seems rent and deracinated, his entire sense of order and unity cracked, split, torn from its fixture. When Agamemnon had asked, 'Is this the lady Cressid?', Diomedes without hesitation had confirmed it, 'Even she' (IV.v. 17). But Troilus, in making his Hamlet-like 'recordation' of 'every syllable that here was spoke', at first refuses to credit what he has heard and seen: 'Was Cressid here?' Desolately rejecting Ulysses' dry retort ('I cannot conjure Troyan'), he insists that 'she was not, sure./... Let it not be believ'd ... / ...Rather think this not Cressid':

> This she? No; this is Diomed's Cressida.
> If beauty have a soul, this is not she;
> If souls guide vows, if vows be sanctimonies,
> If sanctimony be the gods' delight,

If there be rule in unity itself,
This was not she.

(V.ii. 135–40)

But despite his saying that 'my negation hath no taste of madness', that taste of 'plague and madness' floods and overwhelms his mind. He expresses it in poetry more contorted in its anguish than any other in the play, and to which Hazlitt's comment on Ulysses' earlier 'Time' speech equally well applies: 'The throng of images ... is prodigious; and though [or indeed *because*] they ... jostle against one another, they every where raise and carry on the feeling, which is intrinsically true and profound' (*Characters of Shakespeare's Plays*, 1817):

> O madness of discourse,
> That cause sets up with and against itself!
> Bifold authority! where reason can revolt
> Without perdition, and loss assume all reason
> Without revolt: this is, and is not, Cressid.
> Within my soul there doth conduce a fight
> Of this strange nature, that a thing inseparate
> Divides more wider than the sky and earth;
> And yet the spacious breadth of this division
> Admits no orifex for a point as subtle
> As Ariachne's broken woof to enter.
> Instance, O instance! strong as Pluto's gates:
> Cressid is mine, tied with the bonds of heaven.
> Instance, O instance! strong as heaven itself:
> The bonds of heaven are slipp'd, dissolv'd, and loos'd;
> And with another knot, five-finger-tied,
> The fractions of her faith, orts of her love,
> The fragments, scraps, the bits, and greasy relics
> Of her o'er-eaten faith, are bound to Diomed.

(V.ii. 140–58)

'This is, and is not, Cressid'; 'Cressid is *mine* ...' and '...

bound to Diomed': the violent jostling in Troilus' soul makes this indeed a 'supremely difficult' speech, as the notes in the Arden edition help explain, because 'although it attempts to use the language of logic and the methods of rhetoric, it is primarily ... concerned to give utterance to an intolerable state of feeling, and one, moreover, which, by virtue of Troilus' single-minded dedication, is indissolubly linked with his whole moral being.'

'Single', 'indissolubly', 'linked', 'whole': that such terms indeed seem needed to describe the concentrated power of this verse in which Troilus voices his experience of finding all he knew and relied on shattered, 'slipp'd, dissolv'd, and loos'd', is a paradox that takes us to the centre of Shakespeare's achievement here, and more broadly in the play as a whole. Troilus' 'moral being' at this moment expresses in extreme form the strain and turmoil of a mind alive to absolute contradictions in its own nature because they are there in the reality it confronts and must answer to. In this he epitomises that state of soul or mode of human being which in mild and moderate and extreme degrees *Troilus and Cressida* itself not merely expresses but probes and evaluates: a way of experiencing the world as radically paradoxical and contradictory, and of opening one's 'whole moral being' to it without the protection of any guaranteed objective values, any certainties and comforting presuppositions on which to rely: in short, a way of realising the world and answering to it—making moral sense of it—not *despite* the mind's discovery of such paradoxes and contradictions, but in and through the raw experience of these.

Like Troilus, the play has come a long way since it first aroused our laughter over the comical clichés of its opening lines: 'Why should I war without the walls of Troy/That find such cruel battle here within?' And just as the reality of strife 'within' has acquired new meaning, so does the drama now come to realise what is at issue in the war outside the city walls.

(vi)

Unlike Helen's faithlessness to Menelaus, Cressida's betrayal of Troilus does not change the history of the world. For Troilus personally, the significance of her 'change' is immense, and the play gives full weight to it. It also foreshadows impending woe in Cressida's own life as she glances beyond the time when Diomedes will discard her (Troilus 'lov'd me better than you will') to a still more desolate future ('O Jove ... I shall be plagu'd'), when—as Henryson expressed it in his sombre and moving sequel to Chaucer's 'litel ... tragedye', *The Testament of Cresseid*,—she will find herself 'destitute/Of all comfort and consolatioun'. Like Henryson, Shakespeare directs attention to the 'comforts' that people seek and may fail to find for their desolation. Troilus, amidst the death of his hopes, does not conclude that Cressida 'is not worth what she doth cost' him, not worth the toll of pain. All the passion of his loving is rechannelled into loathing of the man who stole her, and the consolation of revenge becomes his life's primary aim. Thus the play confronts us blow by blow with the unedifying spectacle of Troilus and Diomedes bellowing for each others' blood, roaring for supremacy, even after Troilus has shredded the letter from the Cressida who still feeds his hopes but 'edifies another with her deeds'. (He needs no Charon now, no longer 'stay[s] for waftage'—his hatred of Diomedes alone gives him sufficient 'swift transportance': 'Fly not; for shouldst thou take the river Styx/I would swim after') (V.iv. 18–19).

But while the play distinguishes between the issues of this love-affair and the war over Helen, and while it also fully weighs the analogy between them, its closing scenes insist on the relatively far greater importance of the latter. Where Cressida's betrayal involved only those most nearly concerned in it, the life and death of the whole Trojan civilisation is at stake in the question of Hector's survival or his fall. 'The glory of our Troy doth this day lie/On his fair worth and single chivalry'; Troy's first hope is 'fairly built' on Hector, he is the 'base and pillar' of 'yonder city', its 'heart', 'sinews' and 'bone'. And nowhere is the complete dependency of other lives on his made more piteously plain than in the one sight we have of him 'at home', in Troy, in Act V Scene iii.

For here there is no question of love constraining 'half Hector' to 'stay at home'—the whole of him is determined on rushing out to war. In Act I Scene ii, when 'rous'd with rage' by Ajax he was said to have rushed forth before dawn to mow down Greeks, and 'every flower/Did as a prophet weep what it foresaw/In Hector's wrath'. Now it is his wife, sister, father, who weep what they foresee in his wrath. That earlier scene also told of how he had 'chid Andromache, and struck his armourer' before dashing to the field (as 'with a bridegroom's fresh alacrity': cf. IV.iv. 144), 'like as there were husbandry in war' (I.ii. 6ff); now again he chides his wife, again demonstrates his priorities in 'husbandry' by ordering her out of his way. This brief battle of wills is among the most momentous in the play, and the drama here in its pathos and its unsentimental tough-mindedness is reminiscent of other cross-purpose encounters between husband and wife in earlier plays—Kate and Hotspur in *Henry IV, Part One* (II.iii), for instance, and more similarly, Portia and Brutus, and Calphurnia and Caesar in *Julius Caesar* (e.g. II.i; II.ii). But the ironies here are even more knotted and more wrenching than in those.

The inclusion of this incident is all the more important because it works both with and against the Thersitean view that this world holds 'nothing but lechery'. Indeed, Thersites' mirthful contempt is heard to 'croak like a raven'—'Lechery! lechery! Still wars and lechery! Nothing else holds fashion ...'—immediately before this scene opens with Andromache voicing her 'woman's longing' for Hector to remain in Troy, safe, unarmed, in his weeds of peace. The juxtaposition accentuates Andromache's solicitude as something else than lechery—and something whose value cannot be judged merely in terms of its outcome (as 'such and no other than event doth form it'), because its worth is not circumscribed by its efficacy or inefficacy in opposing the vehemence of a Hector for whom at this moment nothing else holds fashion but war. Troilus had earlier described himself as 'weaker than a woman's tear' (I.i. 9), and indeed all the tears in this play, men's tears and women's, are 'weak', unavailing, all too able (in Patroclus' words) to be 'shook to ... air' 'like a dew-drop from the lion's mane' (cf. III.iii. 224). But although such marks of 'weakness' and 'frailty' are always thus set over against contrary 'strengths' and 'powers', they are not thereby proven merely feeble, foolish, worthless, absurd. That is how Thersites views all woe, of course. He admits no such distinctions as the play itself makes and explores; but partly because it does thus admit into its imagination this fact that nothing can shake *his* moral certainties from their fixture, its implicit valuation of distress such as Andromache's is both more inclusive and more compelling than his reductive view. For in this scene, as elsewhere, human tears—and indeed the very capacity to weep—signify loss, defeat, grievous impotence; yet they also evince the strength, the sheer tenacity, the *un*changeful potency, of human attachments: the capacity for loving, desiring, valuing, distinguishing, which is no less basic a part of human nature than the fitful appetites of war and lechery that Thersites sees everywhere he looks.

'The gods have heard me swear', cries Hector; and despite Cassandra's unfaltering attack on his logic—'the gods are deaf to hot and peevish vows'; 'It is the purpose that makes strong the vow;/But vows to every purpose must not hold'—his will is fixed, no more movable by her petitions than by Andromache's. (Here the Folio text gives the latter some (much-disputed) additional lines whose argumentative urgency forecasts Helena's in *All's Well*, and (more strikingly) Isabella's in *Measure* and Hermione's in *The Winter's Tale*, though it cuts less ice with Hector than

Isabella's with Angelo: 'O, be persuaded! Do not count it holy/To hurt by being just. It is as lawful,/For we would give much, to use violent thefts/And rob in the behalf of charity'). Troilus, in turn, fixed in *his* 'hot and peevish vows', is equally 'deaf', 'against all suit', will not 'be persuaded' by Hector to 'unarm'—any more than he was so persuaded in their last such argument, in the council, which this later scene re-echoes and painfully recalls:

> Now, youthful Troilus, do not these high strains
> Of divination in our sister work
> Some touches of remorse, or is your blood
> So madly hot that no discourse of reason,
> Nor fear of bad success in a bad cause,
> Can qualify the same?
>
> (II.ii. 113–18)

But even though—and partly because—her divinations again work no 'touches of remorse' and no 'touch of consanguinity' in either of her brothers, Cassandra's presence is as dramatically crucial here as there, for it is she who insists most forcefully on what Hector's going will mean:

> Lay hold upon him, Priam, hold him fast;
> He is thy crutch; now if thou lose thy stay,
> Thou on him leaning, and all Troy on thee,
> Fall all together.
>
> (V.iii.59–62)

In keeping the oath that he has sworn, Hector—so his sister contends—is forsaking them, exposing them to infinite dangers, breaking what should be his 'major vow' and obligation of his blood (to guard their safety), in short, betraying kin and country by betraying himself: 'Thou dost thyself and all our Troy deceive'.

Thus, as Cassandra shrills aloud her vision of 'what

follows'—'all cry', 'Hector! Hector's dead! O Hector!'—the
princes turn their backs on Troy, flushed anew with
hazardous and madly hot expectancy of 'so rich advantage
of a promis'd glory/As smiles upon the forehead of this
action' (II.ii. 204). Even in the face of such warnings as these,
Hector is bent on negligence. He gives no more credence to
the idea of his own death or of Troy's destruction than he
did when Ulysses and Achilles prophesied both in Act IV
Scene v: 'Wert thou an oracle to tell me so,/I'd not believe
thee'. But the play undercuts any 'comfort and consolation'
to be found in dry detachment from this ignorant ignoring.
Hector's defiant unbelief, his refusal or incapacity to realise
the imminence of his death and Troy's, not only clears the
way for those catastrophes to fall, it also becomes a
definitive mark of that ordinary mortal humanity wherein
Hector epitomises all of them, and all of us who watch the
play.

(vii)

Dryden thought that *Troilus* lost impetus after its fiery start,
and he remarked that 'the later part of the Tragedy is
nothing but a confusion of Drums and Trumpets,
Excursions and Alarms', a view that has often been echoed
down the centuries, including the twentieth. But when
Agamemnon suspects that his party is veering off course
('We go wrong, we go wrong'), Ajax is there to point out
exactly where they are heading: 'No, yonder 'tis;/There,
where we see the lights', and Hector is told that Achilles
'here comes himself to guide you'. And for the audience too,
if we follow the guide and keep our eye on the lights, there is
no question of the play being slack or confused or 'going
wrong' in Act V. It never deviates, but thrusts on forward
through all the obscurities and confusions of its closing
scenes, with a sense of purpose as absolute and
uncompromising as Achilles' own:

> Where is this Hector?
> Come, come, thou boy-queller, show thy face;
> Know what it is to meet Achilles angry.
> Hector! where's Hector? I will none but Hector.
>
> (V.v. 44–7)

'Know what it is to meet Achilles angry': at this scene's opening the Greeks themselves know what it is to meet the Trojans angry, Hector above all. Confusion is everywhere; panic is fanned by shocking facts and no less shocking rumours; the Greeks now for the first time are 'spongy to suck in the sense of fear,/ ... ready to cry out "Who knows what follows?".' Once, they were 'orgillous', 'fresh', 'unbruised'; now, many are 'pashed', 'slain', 'deadly hurt', 'ta'en, or slain',

> Sore hurt and bruis'd. The dreadful Sagittary
> Appals our numbers. Haste we, Diomed,
> To reinforcement, or we perish all.
>
> (V.v. 14–16)

At the start of the play the war's violence had barely (and then only rarely) seemed real; it was held at a distance, viewed as 'sport'—as by Pandarus in Act I Scene ii:

> That's Hector, that, that, look you, that....
> There's a brave man, niece ... Look how he
> looks.... It does a man's heart good. Look you
> what hacks are on his helmet! Look you
> yonder, do you see? ... There's no jesting. ...
> There be hacks.
>
> Cressida Be those with swords?
> Pandarus Swords! anything, he cares not; an the devil
> come to him, it's all one. By God's lid, it does
> one's heart good.
>
> (I.ii. 190–8, *et seq.*)

'Look you yonder, do you see?': the Pandarus who thus
manically looks and looks at the marks of violence but sees
only badges of bravery that warm the cockles of his heart is
himself the one who makes a distinction between different
kinds of degrees of 'knowing':

> *Pandarus* You know me, do you not?
> *Servant*   Faith, sir, superficially.
> *Pandarus* Friend, know me better: I am the Lord
>   Pandarus.
>
> (III.i. 9–11)

It is typical of Shakespeare's procedure to underline, via
apparently trivial comic banter, a distinction which in fact
governs the way the play is progressively organised. For this
distinction between knowing something 'superficially' and
coming to know it 'better', or between knowing 'but partly'
and knowing 'wholly' (i.e. coming fully to *realise* it) is
brought home more and more forcibly by the drama's
gathering intensity during the later Acts. It applies to all of
the Greeks and Trojans and what they do and do not realise
as the action proceeds; but it applies even more to the
audience and what the play impels *us* to realise as we watch.

In Act V Scene v the appalling catalogues of their dead
and wounded certainly make the Greeks—and us—unable
now to evade the reality of these 'hacks' and gashes, made by
'a thousand Hectors' carving a passage through their men
with careless force:

> *Ulysses*   O, courage, courage, Princes! Great Achilles
>   Is arming, weeping, cursing, vowing
>   vengeance.
>   Patroclus' wounds have rous'd his drowsy
>   blood,
>   Together with his mangled Myrmidons,

> That noseless, handless, hack'd and chipp'd,
>   come to him,
> Crying on Hector.
>
> (V.v. 30–5)

This is the nightmare reality on the other side of the
dream of triumph—the hideous injuries men suffer in war as
the cost of those they seek to inflict: 'Noseless, handless,
hack'd and chipp'd: these Myrmidons are precisely *not* 'like
broken statues' (as the Oxford edition has it, p. 34) but
'mangled', maimed, living men who 'have cognition/Of
what [they] feel'. Patroclus, horribly 'hack'd', is dead. As
the frailty of human souls had been realised nowhere more
fully than in Cressida's betrayal and in Troilus'
vulnerability to those 'gashes' of love, so now and
throughout these later scenes the play exposes the terrible
frailty of the human body. And in this image of Achilles—
'*arming, weeping, cursing,* vowing vengeance./Patroclus'
wounds have rous'd his drowsy blood ...'—the connection
is very clear between the frailty of Patroclus' body and the
value Achilles finds and invests in it, between Patroclus'
common, killable humanity and his particular and
irreplaceable significance for his friend. Equally clear, too, is
the connection between that vulnerability, which Achilles
weeps, and the savage drive to avenge it in kind by
slaughtering the killer.

The contrast could hardly be more extreme than between
the bewildering noise, the turmoil of violent energies in this
and surrounding scenes, and the slow orderly intellectual
debates in the Greek and Trojan councils, between the
rhetoric of glory and miseries such as these. And it is in this
incongruence between men's most primitive drives,
emotions and appetites and the civilised ideas and ideals by
which they seek to regulate their lives that the play finds the
immediate 'cause' of Hector's undoing.

One thread in the great knot of ironies here is that by
fatally wounding Patroclus (as 'none but' he is presumed to

have done), Hector has at last achieved what his challenge in
Act I Scene iii had been aimed at—to 'rouse a Grecian that is
true in love', the very one he had sought to rouse. Achilles,
of all the Greeks (as we see it, at least), is the one both most
and least like him: renowned as their greatest warrior, but—
(unlike Hector) hardly known for 'courtesy', 'chivalry',
civility, nor one to indulge in 'magnanimous deeds' or any
'vice of mercy'—least of all towards Hector himself, as Act
IV Scene v amply shows. At his peril will Hector ever ignore
or forget this difference between them, and 'presume on'
Achilles' chivalry where none exists, or forget that his own
chivalry might be far less self-evident and less pure, perfect,
virtuous, than he loves to think. Troilus chides him for his
'*vice* of mercy', but Hector will hear none of it, and their
quarrel here draws attention to all that is at hazard.

For Troilus' phrase is not left unquestioned by the
dramatist who in *The Merchant of Venice*, for instance, had
examined what the *lack* of 'the quality of mercy' might
mean, and who in *Measure for Measure* was to imagine his
heroine powerfully urging the virtue of letting mercy
temper justice. Yet where those plays scrutinised social
customs, laws and institutions in time of peace, these closing
scenes in *Troilus* concern a world of war, in which (so
Troilus insists) distinctions between honour and shame,
justice and injustice, 'fair play' and 'foul' no longer obtain,
and in which it is sheer 'fool's play' to act as if they did. War
makes 'mercy' a 'vice'. In 'weighing well' the implications of
such a view, however, the play clearly does not make a
virtue of bloody-mindedness, nor surrender its own powers
of mind to mindless nihilism: it does not 'lose distinction'
between the value of humane and civilised ideals, however
imperfectly embodied, and the chaos of lawless appetite.
Nor, on the other hand, does it let the principle of 'mercy'
stand as the proper name for what impels Hector to act as he
does; and (as Act V makes plain) it certainly does not show
him to so act consistently. Nestor admiringly recalls him in
battle, 'Despising many forfeits and subduements,/When

thou hast hung thy advanced sword i'th' air,/Not letting it decline on the declined', and Ulysses reports that 'Hector in his blaze of wrath subscribes/To tender objects'. But such 'tender' 'mercy' alternates with the ruthless bouts of 'boy-quelling' as the butcher Hector makes his way 'through ranks of Greekish youth'. Nestor's word 'despising' suggests that Hector's forfeiture of forfeits has less to do with 'mercy' than with a prized self-image, a sense of his own dignity and what it will not stoop to—as indeed his sparing of the 'filthy rogue' Thersites in Act V Scene iv confirms. Troilus had urged 'let's leave the hermit Pity with our mother', and pity and mercy do indeed seem often 'left at home', even when Hector is, as he claims, 'to-day i' th' vein of chivalry' (V.iii. 32).

Thus, as well as inquiring how this 'today' of Hector's relates to 'yesterday' and 'tomorrow', the play probes under the surfaces of such chivalry, and it also (as the metaphor here draws us to notice) examines what else there is in Hector's veins that gets mixed up with it. For as in each and all of these people (and, the play implies, in each of us) the blood that courses through Hector's veins—the very 'sap' of his being—is a 'commixtion'; and in his case, as the iteration of Agamemnon's metaphor suggests, the mixture or conflux of impulses in him seems bound to prove disastrous: 'checks and disasters/Grow in the veins .../As knots, by the conflux of meeting sap, / Infects the sound pine ...' (I.iii. 5–8).

It is in this context that Shakespeare introduces the business of the knight in sumptuous armour who happens to cross Hector's path and is mercilessly hunted to death. The incident derives from Lydgate (in Book III of his *Troy Book*), who characteristically moralises here about the 'greedy fret' of false covetousness. Most commentators agree on the unlikelihood of Shakespeare's intending a similarly simple moralistic lesson, but the incident is strange even so—especially because of Hector's sententious moral handwashing once the job is done:

Most putrified core, so fair without,
Thy goodly armour thus hath cost thy life.

                                        (V.viii. 1–2)

This idea of man having a fair outside and a rotten interior
was a central one in *Hamlet*, of coure, and on Shakespeare's
mind in earlier plays, but *Troilus* discovers fresh life in it, as
it does in Diomedes' attack on Helen's 'contaminated
carrion weight', and in exposing here some of the ins and
outs of Hector's 'chivalry'.

The moral thinking evinced in the play's conception of
this brief incident cuts beneath Hector's own complacent
moralising to focus on the paradox of his second line, that
this 'goodly armour' worn for *protection* has actually cost its
wearer his life. The instant Hector first caught sight of the
sumptuous outfit, he desired to possess it himself: the
defensive gear excited the predation it was meant to prevent.
The headlong savagery of Hector's appetite expresses
something far in excess of mere greed for possession: 'I'll
frush it [smash it] and unlock the rivets all /But I'll be master
of it' (V.vi. 29–30). The lust to dominate, to overpower, the
thrill of *mastering*, is itself both the primary drive and the
primary aim or object, possession of the sumptuous armour
merely the sign and symbol of *that*: the satisfaction is to
smash, to unlock all those rivets, to prove one's absolute
supremacy, 'sans check'. Yet while the play thus underlines
the irony of deterrents acting as provocations, it sets this
against a contrary irony, whereby voluntary *dis*armament
not only fails to guarantee the enemy's reciprocal pacifism
but provides him with an opportunity that may prove
irresistible, to attack exactly when the quarry is unarmed.

'Call here my varlet; I'll unarm again ...' (I.i. 1): from its
very first lines and recurrently throughout, the play draws
attention to the physical actions of arming and disarming,
and to the appetites and vulnerabilities they symbolise, as
not only in Troilus or in Achilles, but even more in the
Hector ('arm'd, and bloody in intent') who spurns the plea

that he 'unarm, unarm, and do not fight to-day'—the same
Hector of whom, when he came back safe in Act 3, Paris had
said,

> Sweet Helen, I must woo you
> To help unarm our Hector. His stubborn buckles,
> With these your white enchanting fingers touch'd,
> Shall more obey than to the edge of steel
> Or force of Greekish sinews; you shall do more
> Than all the island kings—disarm great Hector.
> (III.i. 142–7)

'Where is this Hector?/ ... /Know what it is to meet
Achilles angry': Hector armed or unarmed makes no odds
to Achilles now. It's not just the 'hide' Achilles is hunting
but the 'core' he means to 'frush'; and when Hector lets him
pause, he disdains this courtesy, saying, 'My rest and
negligence befriends thee now,/But thou anon shalt hear of
me again'. But Hector is hard of hearing, wrapt in his own
ideas and concerns, and he knows Achilles' wrath but
'superficially'. Even now he neglects to grasp that his own
'rest and negligence' might 'anon' 'befriend' his foe: *I would
have been* much more a fresher man,/*Had I expected thee*
(V.vi. 20–1, my italics). Such non-expectancy is perilous
enough, but it is nothing beside the hazard of his expectation
that Achilles is governed by a code of 'honour' like his own:

Hector   Rest, sword; thou hast thy fill of blood and
          death!

                              [*Disarms*]

Priam had prayed that 'The gods with safety stand about
thee'. But against that hope the play pits the appalling image
of Hector suddenly 'rounded in with danger'; instead of
'safety' to 'stand about him' comes Achilles, with his gang of
Myrmidons:

Achilles	Look, Hector, how the sun begins to set;
	How ugly night comes breathing at his heels;
	Even with the vail and dark'ning of the sun,
	To close the day up, Hector's life is done.
Hector	I am unarm'd; forego this vantage, Greek.
Achilles	Strike, fellows, strike; this is the man I seek.

[*Hector falls*]
(V.vii. 5–10)

Isn't this the end we have expected all along? In a sense it
is. But the hideous shock of the killing shows the real answer
to be 'No'. We had foreseen that the outcome would be
bloody, but our imagination had not prepared us for how it
would taste indeed. We were not forearmed against this
gloryless brutality. It is as if we too have been ambushed,
taken by surprise—betrayed, lured into the security of
supposing we know 'what follows', only to find we had been
ignorant, unwitting, that even here our expectation has set
all on hazard. The play has seduced us, goaded us to
'prenominate in nice conjecture' how it would end: 'Hector
the great must die'. Yet it seems we knew it but
'superficially', supposing his death would be the great
climax of the war. That he should die unarmed, not even in
battle, not even by Achilles' hand? We had not realised—
not even imagined—such possibilities as these.

Full of hypotheses, surmises, suppositions—another
aspect of its famed 'modernity'—the play has roused in our
minds, as in the minds of the Greeks and Trojans, endless
speculations about 'what's yet in the word "hereafter"'; but
at the last—and suddenly—it throws us out of that safer
realm of 'if', 'perhaps', 'maybe', 'what will it be, when …?',
into the realm of this actuality, no longer provisional or
hypothetical, but immediate and real. All chance of some
other 'if' is 'frushed' along with Hector.

What significance does this absolute fact of Hector's
death have in the play? In what spirit does the play
foreshadow the inevitable destruction of Troy?

Part of an answer is bound up in the play's uncompromising insistence that even in this death there are no objective or incontestable values. The various Greeks and Trojans regard the event in quite contrary ways: for some, it is an immitigable tragedy; for others (Achilles, Pandarus) it is nothing of the kind. And the drama that expresses and stresses all these divergent valuations, comprehending all of them in its totality, cannot without distortion be equated with any one, because even now it centres in the strife, the oppugnancy, between them. In a pointed omission, no formal encomium is made over the butchered body, nothing resembling Hal's (albeit self-congratulatory) acknowledgement of Hotspur's worth, for example, or the tributes paid by the victors to the vanquished near the end of *Julius Caesar* or *Antony and Cleopatra* or *Coriolanus*. Stunned by the facts, even Troilus (in whom Troy puts its second hope) can only repeat over and over what Cassandra had said in her desperate pre-mortem obituary: 'Hector is slain', 'Hector is gone. Who shall tell Priam so, or Hecuba?', 'Hector's dead', 'Hector is dead'. Troilus' despair momentarily disintegrates into the emotional nihilism that comes when no fresh appetite or hope for life is left. As for Achilles, he has no regrets. He concedes that Hector is 'mighty' only because this proves himself still mightier; to him, 'the Troyan' is a tasty morsel rather than a square meal; and his rage to avenge Patroclus' death seems forgotten amidst the more basic pleasure of providing a snack for his long-starved sword: 'My half-supp'd sword, that frankly would have fed,/Pleas'd with this dainty bait, thus goes to bed.' Far from respecting, let alone sharing, the Trojans' sense of the sanctity of the dead hero's body, Achilles will drag it along the field, a carcase whose only value is in signifying his well-earned triumph.

And even here, when every heroic ideal is annihilated, the play scants and famishes our desire for moral simplicity, and rudely beguiles our lips of all rejoinder. Though Troilus, his spirit almost broken, says, 'Hector is dead.

There is no more to say', the play finds something more for
its 'notorious bawd' to say—gives him, indeed, its final
words, at the uttermost remove from epic grandeur. It puts a
violent sting in its tail for anyone who yearns for some
sweeter notes of comfort or consolation, as the clapped-out
Pandarus sings unmerrily of the merry humble bee when
'sweet honey and sweet notes together fail', and at last
departs (like us) to 'seek about for eases' to the 'diseases'
bequeathed to us by such an ending.

The apprehension in *Troilus* of life's rude brevity is far
more terse than that in any of Shakespeare's previous plays,
devoid of all the harmoniously elegiac notes of *Twelfth
Night* ('Youth's a stuff will not endure') or *Henry IV, Part
One* ('O gentlemen, the time of life is short!'), or the open-
stopped pathos of the closing scene of *Hamlet*. When
Troilus despairs, Aeneas says, 'My lord, you do discomfort
all the host'; and the play itself in its closing scenes seems
aimed maximally to discomfort all the host of its audience.
Part of what makes this final Act so abrasive, so shelterless—
and again, so 'modern'—is that the 'chance of war' and the
chance of love are here entirely a matter of human actions,
not godly interventions. And this fact that the gods or God
never enter into it (except tangentially, via occasional
prayers) goes a long way to crystallise the main differences in
feeling and outlook between *Troilus* and Homer's poem on
the one hand and Chaucer's on the other. There is no sense
here that the world is held in a providential hand, nor that
losses can be redeemed, nor that there is some ultimate
plane of extra-temporal reality in which we might stand and
observe and evaluate all that happens. By contrast with the
older poems, Troilus is fiercer, far more raw. Yet although
its spirit, especially at the end, may seem on the face of it to
have little in common with that of either *The Iliad* or *Troilus
and Criseyde*, the affinity of all three is focused in their sense
that the value of human lives is not nullified by their
ultimate ruin but positively 'declared', fully realised, in the
facts of loss and death. The drama neither expresses nor

induces a wry 'so what?' cynicism nor any version of nihilism; its 'effect doth operate another way'. For while it compels our assent to the lethal logic of Hector's assassination of Patroclus, or the Myrmidons' of Hector, it simultaneously compels our feelings to *dissent* from such things. These lives are fragile, they do not last; but that does not mean that we acquiesce in their extinction. As the Myrmidons close in and Achilles cries, 'Be't so', the play 'wakes [us] to answer', 'No'.

'Look, Hector, ...', Achilles says, and it is not just Hector but we who must look at the sight of ugly night '*breathing*' at the heels of the setting sun. There is evil in nature, in human nature, that we can no more evade than Hector can, or Patroclus, or the Trojans whose doom it spells. Yet our realisation of its cost in sheer waste of life provokes a resistent counter-energy of desire—'*would it were otherwise!*'—even as the play confronts us with this image of 'our sure destructions', and 'the frailty of our powers'. Because it compels the realisation that all these Greek and Trojan lives will be grated to dusty nothing, the ending defies us to ignore our 'touch of consanguinity' with all of them. It is not despite but because of the ultimate facts of death that human beings need to construct—and fight over—meaning and value.

Select Bibliography

(i) TEXTS

Alexander   *William Shakespeare, The Complete Works*, ed. Peter Alexander, London 1951.

Arden   *Troilus and Cressida*, ed. Kenneth Palmer, new *Arden Shakespeare*, London and New York 1982.

First Folio   *The First Folio of Shakespeare*, ed. Charlton Hinman (The Norton Facsimile), New York 1968.

Honigmann   E. A. J. Honigmann, 'The Date and Revision of *Troilus and Cressida*', in *Textual Criticism and Literary Interpretation*, ed. Jerome J. McGann, Chicago 1985.

New Cambridge *Troilus and Cressida*, ed. Alice Walker, *New Cambridge Shakespeare*, Cambridge 1957.

New Penguin   *Troilus and Cressida*, ed. R. A. Foakes, *New Penguin Shakespeare*, Harmondsworth 1987.

New Variorum   *Troilus and Cressida*, ed. H. N. Hillebrand, *New Variorum Shakespeare*, Philadelphia and London 1953.

Quarto	*Troilus and Cressida*, in Shakespeare Quarto Facsimile series, no.8, Oxford 1952.
Oxford	*Troilus and Cressida*, ed. Kenneth Muir, *The Oxford Shakespeare*, Oxford 1982.
Oxford	*William Shakespeare, The Complete Works*, gen. eds. Stanley Wells and Gary Taylor, Oxford 1986.
Riverside	*The Riverside Shakespeare*, textual ed. G. Blakemore Evans, Boston 1974; introduction to *Troilus and Cressida* by Anne Barton.
Signet	*Troilus and Cressida*, ed. Daniel Seltzer, *Signet Classic*, New York 1963.
Taylor	Gary Taylor, 'Troilus and Cressida: Bibliography, Performance and Interpretation', *Shakespeare Studies* XV (1982), pp.99–136.

(ii) SOURCE-MATERIALS

Bullough	Geoffrey Bullough, *Narrative and Dramatic Sources of Shakespeare*, vol. 6, London and New York 1966.
Chapman	*Chapman's Homer*, ed. Allardyce Nicholl, 2 vols, London 1957.
Chaucer	*The Works of Geoffrey Chaucer*, ed. F. N. Robinson, London 1957.
Donaldson	E. Talbot Donaldson, *The Swan at the Well: Shakespeare Reading Chaucer*, New Haven and London 1985.
Henryson	*Robert Henryson—Poems*, ed. Charles Elliott, Oxford 1963.
Homer	*The Iliad of Homer*, trans. Richmond Lattimore, Chicago and London 1951.

Kimbrough Robert Kimbrough, *Shakespeare's 'Troilus and Cressida' and Its Setting*, Cambridge, Mass. 1964.

Muir Kenneth Muir, *The Sources of Shakespeare's Plays*, London 1977.

Thompson Ann Thompson, *Shakespeare's Chaucer: A Study in Literary Origins*, Liverpool 1978.

(iii) STAGE-HISTORY AND CRITICAL RECEPTION

Arnold Margaret J. Arnold, '"Monsters in Love's Train": Euripides and Shakespeare's *Troilus and Cressida*', *Comparative Drama* 18 (1984) pp. 38–53.

Bayley John Bayley, *The Uses of Division*, London 1976.

Berman Ronald Berman, *A Reader's Guide to Shakespeare's Plays*, Glenview, Illinois 1965.

Berry Ralph Berry, *Shakespeare and the Awareness of the Audience*, London 1985.

Bevington David Bevington, *Shakespeare*, Golden Tree Bibliography, New York 1978.

Cole Douglas Cole, 'Myth and Anti-Myth: The Case of *Troilus and Cressida*', *Shakespeare Quarterly* 31 (1980) pp. 76–84.

Coleridge *S. T. Coleridge: Shakespearean Criticism*, ed. Thomas Middleton Raysor, 2 vols, London and New York 1960, vol. 1, pp. 97–100.

Dollimore Jonathan Dollimore, *Radical Tragedy*, Brighton 1984.

Dryden *Troilus and Cressida, Or, Truth Found Too*

	Late (1679), Facsimile by Cornmarket Press, London 1969.
Dusinberre	Juliet Dusinberre, 'Troilus and Cressida and the Definition of Beauty', *Shakespeare Survey* 36 (1983) pp. 85–95.
Everett	Barbara Everett, 'The Inaction of *Troilus and Cressida*, in *Essays in Criticism*, 32 (1982) pp. 119–39.
Fermor	Una Ellis Fermor, *The Frontiers of Drama*, London 1945.
Fly	Richard D. Fly, *Shakespeare's Mediated World*, Amherst 1976.
Freund	Elizabeth Freund, '"Ariachne's Broken Woof": The Rhetoric of Citation in *Troilus and Cressida*', in *Shakespeare and the Question of Theory*, ed. P. Parker and G. Hartman, New York and London 1985.
Green	Lawrence D. Green, '"We'll Dress Him Up in Voices": The Rhetoric of Disjunction in *Troilus and Cressida*', *Quarterly Journal of Speech* 70 (1984), pp. 23–40.
Greene	Gayle Greene, 'Shakespeare's Cressida', in *The Woman's Part*, ed. C. Lenz, G. Greene and C. Neely, Urbana, Chicago and London 1980.
Johnson	*Johnson on Shakespeare*, ed. Arthur Sherbo, The Yale edition of *The Works of Samuel Johnson*, vol. VIII, New Haven and London 1968.
Jones	Emrys Jones, *Scenic Form in Shakespeare*, Oxford 1971.
Hazlitt	*The Complete Works of William Hazlitt*, ed. P. P. Howe, vol. 4, London and Toronto 1930.
Helton	Tinsley Helton, 'Paradox and Hypothesis in *Troilus and Cressida*', *Shakespeare*

	Studies X (1977) pp.115–31.
Knight	G. Wilson Knight, *The Wheel of Fire*, Oxford 1930.
Langman	F. H. Langman, '*Troilus and Cressida*', in *Jonson and Shakespeare*, ed. Ian Donaldson, London 1983, pp.57–73.
Long	Michael Long, *The Unnatural Scene*, London 1976.
Martin	Priscilla Martin, ed., *Troilus and Cressida: A Casebook*, London 1976.
McAlindon	T. McAlindon, 'Language, Style and Meaning in *Troilus and Cressida*', PMLA 84 (1969) pp.29–43.
Morris	Brian Morris, 'The Tragic Structure of *Troilus and Cressida*', *Shakespeare Quarterly* 10 (1959) pp.481–91.
Muir	Kenneth Muir, '*Troilus and Cressida*', *Shakespeare Survey* 8 (1955) pp.28–39.
Newlin	Jeanne T. Newlin, 'The Modernity of *Troilus and Cressida*: The Case for Theatrical Criticism', *Harvard Library Bulletin* 17 (1969) pp.353–73.
Richards	I. A. Richards, '*Troilus and Cressida* and Plato' [1948]; reprinted in his *Speculative Instruments*, Chicago and London 1955.
Rossiter	A. P. Rossiter, *Angel With Horns*, London 1961.
Smith et al.	*Self and Society in Shakespeare: Essays on 'Troilus and Cressida' and 'Measure for Measure'*, University of Leeds' Bradford Centre Occasional Papers, no.4, 1982.
Stein	Arnold Stein, '*Troilus and Cressida*: The Disjunctive Imagination', *English Literary History*, 36 (1969) pp.145–67.
Sprigge	Douglas Sprigge, 'Shakespeare's Visual Stagecraft: The Seduction of Cressida', in *Shakespeare: The Theatrical Dimension*, ed.

P. McGuire and D. Samuelson, New York 1979, pp. 148–63.

Swinburne   A. C. Swinburne, *A Study of Shakespeare*, London [1880] 1929.

Wheeler   Richard Wheeler, *Shakespeare's Development and the Problem Comedies*, Berkeley 1981.

Wilders   John Wilders, 'The Problem Comedies', in *Shakespeare: Select Bibliographical Guides*, ed. Stanley Wells, Oxford 1973, pp. 94–112.

Index

172